Child-Sensitive TEACHING

Karyn Henley

Child-Sensitive TEACHING

Helping children grow a living faith in a loving God

Library of Congress Cataloging-in-Publication Data
Henley, Karyn.
Child-sensitive teaching : helping children grow a living faith in a loving God / by Karyn Henley.
p. cm.
Originally published: Nashville, Tenn. : Allen Thomas Pub., 1993.
Includes bibliographical references.
ISBN 0-7847-0696-4
1. Christian education of children. 2. Christian education—Teaching methods. 3. Christian education—Home training. 4. Child rearing—Religious aspects—Christianity. I. Title.
[BV1475.2.H46 1997]
268' .432—dc21 97-6391
CIP

Cover design: B-LIN
Inside illustrations: Joe Stites
Project editor: Ruth Frederick
Typography: Sherry F. Willbrand

The Standard Publishing Company, Cincinnati, Ohio
A division of Standex International Corporation

04 03 02 01 00 99 98 97 5 4 3 2 1

Contents

Communication in the Classroom

The Growing Teacher

Introduction

The sign on the wall next to the Sunday school classroom said,

"Teachers are invited guests.
Parents are the real teachers."

Whether you are the parent or the classroom teacher, the challenge remains the same. How do we guide our children into a strong and lasting relationship with God our Father, with his Son, Jesus, and with his Holy Spirit? The question is all about communication. How can we communicate most effectively, not just about God, but with God?

Teaching is not just dispensing information, it's touching lives. It's not just managing a classroom or a household, it's uncovering the path to eternal life. It's throwing open the doors to God's kingdom and saying, "Have you met my Father? Have you met his Son? Isn't he wonderful?! Let's go in together and get to know him better!"

There are many factors for a teacher to think about: curriculum, methods, materials, facilities, schedule, co-workers, classroom management techniques. All of these are important, and all of these are covered in this book. But nothing is as important as the child and your relationship with him. That will affect all the other factors and will determine the effectiveness of your communication with him.

Child-Sensitive Teaching focuses on the child and his needs. It looks first at preparing your heart and mind for communicating with children. Then it takes you through practical methods and techniques that will support your communication skills.

But I pray that God will go far beyond the black words on the white pages. I pray that God will guide you deeper into relationship with him and bring to your mind ways to communicate his heart to the specific children you work with each week. I pray that *Child-Sensitive Teaching* will be just a springboard for your own God-given vision and creativity.

The Growing CHILD

Chapter 1

The Child's-Eye View

What's It Like to Be a Child?

"Life is hard. You have to go potty even when you don't want to." —Three year old

Anyone who's spent time with young children knows that they often say and do wonderful things that give us a peek into their minds. I used to write down some of the insights my children, now teenagers, gave me when they were preschoolers. My older son, Raygan, called his echo his "hide-and-seek voice." A nest was a "bird pocket." Wigs were "put-on hairs." A life jacket was a "splashing coat."

While putting on his underpants one day, Raygan began to "read" the tag. "And I will dwell in the house of the Lord forever," he said. When he bit off more peanut butter and jelly sandwich than he could chew, he spit out the whole mouthful and said, "I need another one. This one is dead."

My younger son, Heath, was just as clever. He called his head bone his "skull-a-ton." One day he said, "I'm gonna buy me some new legs. These legs hurt in my flip-flops." Heath saved everything in the refrigerator, which he called the "fwizwator." He put pennies and rocks in there, and even a box of instant oatmeal.

We laugh at a lot of the things children say and do. Sometimes we cry over what they say and do! But if you want to work with children, watching and listening to them is very important. That's because watching and listening to children gives you clues about how they think. You will learn what they understand and what they don't understand. When you know how they think and what they understand, you can better communicate with them.

Children amaze us. Sometimes we stand back, shaking our heads. "This child is off in a world of his own," we say. And that's true. He is.

Do you remember what it was like to be a child? Do you remember what it was like to be misunderstood? What was it like to misunderstand? What was it like to *need* to wiggle? What was it like to feel like dancing? What was it like to be laughed at? What was it like to have to wait? What was it like to watch tiny things and to wonder?

As I've studied the art and craft of writing for children, I've learned that if I want to touch children in a significant way, I must reach into myself and touch my childhood. I have to see through the eyes of the child in me and to write in a way that makes that child laugh or cry or gasp or giggle.

No time is more important to remember what it was like to be a child than when you work with children. Of course, it may not be easy to look back at your childhood. Some childhoods do not make good memories. Some are full of pain, rejection, abuse, and hurt. But even so, there is good reason to remember your past. The good reason is the children who are hurting today. These are some of the same children you will be working with as you teach.

Jesus told Peter, "Simon, Simon, Satan has asked to sift you as wheat. But I have prayed for you, Simon, that your faith may not fail. *And when you have turned back, strengthen your brothers*" (Luke 22:31, 32; emphasis mine). Do you feel like you were sifted in childhood? Strengthen your little brothers and sisters because you understand.

Paul experienced hard times, but he said, "This happened that we might not rely on ourselves but on God" (2 Corinthians 1:9). He also said, "Praise be to the God . . . who comforts us in all our troubles, so that we can comfort those in any trouble with the comfort we ourselves have received from God" (2 Corinthians 1:3, 4).

Even Jesus had hard times. Hebrews 4:15, 16 tells us that Jesus was "a high priest . . . who has been tempted in every way, just as we are. . . . Let us then approach the throne of grace with confidence, so that we may receive mercy and find grace to help us in our time of need."

Jesus wasn't human for nothing. He knows what it's like to get angry. He knows what it's like to be concerned. He know how it feels to be disappointed and even betrayed. He knows what it's like to laugh and cry. He knows what it feels like to be weary. Or to be misunderstood. Or to be laughed at. He knows what it's like to win and lose.

We know these things too. We know what it's like to be a child. We've been there. We weren't kids for nothing. Now children should be able to "receive mercy" from us. They should be able to "find grace to help . . . in [their] time of need."

A Child's World

Let's look now at the world from a child's-eye view. Let's try to remember what it was like.

A child views the world with his own logic.

David Elkind says, "Children are most like us in feeling, least like us in thinking."[1] Children are relatively new in the world. They try to make sense of it the best they can. They respond in ways that are logical to them. But many times, their logic stems from their imagination. All it takes is listening to a child to see that his thoughts are not like yours. In the next few chapters, we'll see more about why this is true. Do you want to communicate well with children? Then listen to them. Hear how they think.

One of my sons called pant legs "leg sleeves." Logical, isn't it? When he was three, he was fascinated by my sewing scissors. They were very sharp, so I kept them in a plastic sheath when he was around. One day he carefully looked them over and then asked, "Can it sizz?" Washers wash, clippers clip, scissors must sizz. Of course! It makes perfect sense.

A child's world is full of possibilities.

In the 1940s, Shinichi Suzuki, a violinist from Japan, developed a method of teaching young children how to play musical instruments. He said, "In the beginner's mind there are many possibilities; in the expert's mind there are few."[2] Children believe that almost anything is possible. They will often say "I can do it" when we have great doubts about whether they really can.

I remember telling my mother that I could carry a pie from the car to the house. The pie didn't make it. Thanks to my mother's grace, I did. Thinking anything is possible in their own strength sometimes gets children into trouble. But it is also one of the motivators that help children learn and accomplish difficult tasks.

A child's world is a mixture of fantasy and reality.

Thinking anything is possible stems in part from a child's active imagination. Until a child is about five years old, he has a hard time distinguishing fantasy from reality. As far as he's concerned, Big Bird is a real friend of his. Barney, the purple dinosaur, can come over and play in the backyard. Animals can talk and action figures can have real adventures. When he goes to sleep at night, the teacups and saucers come out of the cupboards to sing and dance like they do in Disney movies.

One day I was getting ready to run some errands. My preschool son asked, "Mommy, will you do me a favorite? Will you drive by the river and get a duck and bring him home? And if you see a hippopotamus and an elephant, let them ride with you."

Before I had children, I taught at a private preschool in the Los Angeles area. One day we were preparing to grill hot dogs outside. A teacher had begun to light the coals in the grill. One little boy watched intently. Then, pointing to the charcoal, he asked, "Are those gonna turn into hot dogs?" He was watching to see if something magical was going to happen.

Psychologists know that people respond to situations based on their perception of reality, not based on reality itself. A child's world is so steeped in imagination that his reactions are often based on his imagination. So we sometimes see children respond more strongly than we do. The child's response may be overly fearful, worried, or excited. The child's response level and ours may be very different. This is true not only for preschoolers, but for children older than five and for teenagers too.

A child's world is less inhibited than an adult's.
When a child is born, he is completely egocentric. He doesn't worry about what people are going to think of him. He doesn't worry about social conventions or what's proper in front of others. He is very uninhibited. More than one teacher has heard family secrets blurted out in class.

The younger the child, the less inhibited he tends to be. Young children who don't know a word to describe something just make up a word. One four year old said, "I got cookie stuck in the top of my mouth, so I took my tongue and thwooshed it out."

I stood in line at the post office recently and passed the time by watching a little girl who was probably about eighteen months old. Everyone else was watching her too. While her mother waited in line, the little girl climbed on top of and into everything she could find. She pulled large mailing envelopes out of their display and tugged on the ropes that guided the formation of our line. This little one was full of energy and was using as much of it as her mom would allow.

When it was time for the little girl to leave, she waved

good-bye to everyone in line. All of us waved back, except for one man. He was engrossed in his piece of mail. Undaunted and uninhibited, this little girl walked right up to him and waved at his face.

A child's world is full of curiosities.

A child is very aware that there are lots of things he does not know, and he has a natural curiosity to find out about them. If a child doesn't burn out on learning, that desire to learn can stay with him into adulthood.

Four and five year olds are at a prime time in their lives for discovering and learning about their world. At this age, they ask lots of questions. I went on a field trip with my four-year-old class one day. As we rode along, I pointed out interesting sights to the little boy who sat by me on the bus. Suddenly, I spied a flatbed truck carrying an old house.

"Look at that truck moving a house," I said.

My little friend gazed in awe at the house and then asked thoughtfully, "Where are the roots?"

A child's world is often overwhelming.

There's a lot about the adult world that children don't understand, so children may have fears that seem unreasonable to adults. My son wanted the window shades closed when it was dark "so the night won't come in."

The physical scale of a child's world is much bigger to them than our world is to us. Do you remember what it was like to sit in chairs when your feet wouldn't touch the floor? Do you remember not being able to see the top of the kitchen counter? Do you remember standing in a group of grown-ups and looking them squarely in the belt?

Imagine how it would feel if our stairs were proportioned to you the way they are to a child. How high would you have to step? Think of the energy it would take to go up a flight of stairs! A child spends much of his time getting around, over, past, or through the physical obstacles that surround him every day.

But the physical world isn't the only thing that's overwhelming. Along with the rest of us, the child is bombarded every day by all sorts of things vying for his attention. A 1993 report showed that the average American is confronted with 3,000 advertisements a day. That's 1,095,000 ads a year. By the time a child is fifteen, he's seen more than 16,425,000 ads.[3] Each ad tries to be the liveliest, most colorful, loudest, or brightest to catch the attention of the public.

One spring, our symphony gave a children's concert that took us on a tour of music from the beginning of time up until the last years of the twentieth century. The first "music" we heard was from nature—a brook gurgling, birds singing, the wind stirring leaves in the trees, a dog barking.

As each period of music went by, there were more and more instruments, more and more sounds. It progressed until we heard avant-garde music that was a cacophony of machine and traffic sounds along with instruments. The symphony conductor made the comment that in these days, we learn to block out sounds. All day, we shut out peripheral sounds in order to focus on what we're doing.

Is this why I can stand three feet from a child, call his name, and get no response? Maybe he is shutting out sound so he can focus and concentrate on what he's doing.

A child's world is "now."

Adults often talk about how fast time passes. Every year seems to pass faster and faster. I was talking about this to my sixteen-year-old son. "A year *is* shorter to an adult," he said. "Just think about it. To a six year old, a year is one-sixth of his entire life. But to someone forty-six, a year is only one-forty-sixth of his entire life. It's shorter as you get older."

Bypassing these philosophical issues, the reality is that young children do not have the mental capacity to comprehend the flow of time. This ability does not develop until they are about seven or eight years old. So they live in the present. To a young child, "long ago" was yesterday at Grandma's house. You can tell him, "In two weeks, it will be your birthday." But he'll wake up tomorrow and ask, "Is it my birthday yet?" Christmas may be "just around the corner," but it can seem like an eternity to a young child.

A child's world is self-focused.

Children are not born thinking of others. The younger the child, the more naturally self-centered he is. If a baby is cold or hungry or wet or uncomfortable, he usually communicates it immediately. The world revolves around him. He knows nothing else.

As the child grows, he begins to interact with more and more of the world around him. He works at finding out how he affects his world; he gradually begins to see other people's needs. But voluntarily putting others first demands a high level of maturity. This maturity develops as the child's own needs are met. Then he becomes free to reach out and help meet the needs of other people.

Why Study Childhood?

Part of being child-sensitive is trying to see what the world feels like from the child's perspective. That information is valuable to us. First, it helps us to see the child's needs more clearly. Next, it helps us to respect the child. It also helps us to communicate more effectively with the child.

One way to see from the child's viewpoint is to remember what it was like to be a child. Another way is to watch and listen to children. We can also learn from people who have studied children.

Robert Coles, professor of psychiatry and medical humanities at Harvard Medical School, has spent thirty years listening to children. He received a Pulitzer prize for his five-volume *Children of Crisis* series. In an interview, Coles said that children "offer us a chance to see a good part of what we are: human beings struggling to figure out what this world means." We need to "regard children as fellow human beings yet to be constricted and constrained the way that some of us have been as we have made the various compromises that are called growing up," he said. "The point is not to romanticize children but to understand the . . . perspective they have. . . . They are new on the block, so to speak. As a consequence, they have a certain kind of openness of mind and heart."[4]

There's another reason for trying to see the world from a child's viewpoint. Jesus said, "Unless you change and become like little children, you will never enter the kingdom of heaven" (Matthew 18:3). If for no other reason than this, childhood is worth a good, long look. In God's kingdom, we are all children of the Father. So we are children teaching children. We can all rejoice to hear Jesus say, "Let the little children come to me . . . for the kingdom of God belongs to such as these" (Mark 10:14).

Chapter 2

S.O.S. Bear

The Needs of Childhood

The sun was shining as a four year old and his mother went into Kmart.

But while they were shopping, dark clouds gathered and covered the sun.

When the boy and his mom left the store, the little boy said, "Where did God go? He was here a minute ago."

One of our goals as teachers and parents is to help children reach a level of maturity where they put others first. They help. They share. They give. Our hope is that they will serve others because they choose to, not because they're forced to.

At first glance, it might seem that focusing on meeting a child's needs gives too much attention to the child. Won't that keep him centered on himself? No. In fact, just the opposite is true. The child whose needs are met can focus on other people, instead of on his own unfulfilled needs. He doesn't have to spend time trying to get his own needs met.

We are talking about *needs* now, not *wants.* It's possible that what a child wants is also what he needs. But it's quite possible that what he wants is not at all what he needs. That's why one of his greatest needs is adults who can help him make right choices. These adults will not cater to his every want but *will* try to provide for his needs.

Meeting a child's needs also models for him how to help others. Our human tendency is to treat others the way we've been treated. So if we treat a child with respect, he is more likely to treat others with respect. This is the way God deals with us. "We love because he first loved us" (1 John 4:19).

Children's Needs

So what are the needs of children? Their needs include security, optimism, significance, belonging, exploration, the appreciation of childhood, and relationship.

Security

Every child needs a place where he can feel safe and secure. First of all, he needs physical safety. A study from St. Mary's University in San Antonio, Texas, reported that ghosts and darkness no longer rank as the greatest fears of children ages seven to nine years old. Their biggest fears now are rooted in reality: drive-by shootings, kidnappers, gangs, and drugs.[1]

Children also need to feel safe from emotional attack. One of the biggest fears of all people, including children, is the fear of rejection. Yet criticism and mockery pervade our society. We find it easy to laugh at others. The humor in most television sitcoms comes from belittling others. The talk in school classrooms and halls is often centered on cutting others down.

Optimism

Another fear ranks close to the fear of rejection. It's the fear of failure. The child who is afraid to fail is the child who stops trying. Someone may have told him that he'll never make it or that he'll never be good enough, and he believed what he was told. The fear of failure paralyzes people.

Optimism helps to combat the fear of failure. Optimism is believing that things are going to work out for the best. It's the light at the end of the tunnel that helps keep us going when things get tough. Everyone gets discouraged sometimes, but optimism encourages us to see failures and other problems as stepping-stones instead of stumbling blocks. As the saying goes, "When life hands you a lemon, make lemonade."

Children need us to encourage them. They need adults who have a kind sense of humor, adults who can laugh at their own mistakes, adults who are optimistic. Solomon wrote, "Though a righteous man falls seven times, he rises again" (Proverbs 24:16). God's people have every reason to be optimistic. "All things work together for good for them that love God" (Romans 8:28, KJV).

Significance

All people need to feel that they are important to someone. Children are no different. What makes you feel significant? Someone acknowledges your presence, welcomes you, spends time with you, listens to you, values your work and your efforts, asks you to join in their work and their play. When adults notice children, speak to them, listen to them, and call them by name, children feel significant.

People also feel significant when they feel needed. When you are able to help someone else, to serve another person, to do tasks that are productive and meaningful, you feel significant. This is true of children too. As they grow and learn to do more on their own, they feel competent and significant.

Why is feeling significant so important? As one mother said, "When people feel worthless, they act worthless." But when people feel significant, they act as if what they do will be significant. They feel that what they say and do will make a difference. That motivates them to be more responsible. They don't want to jeopardize their self-respect or the respect that others have for them.

So check your attitude toward children. Do you feel that they are a nuisance or are "in the way"? Or are they a treasure to you? Are you glad to get rid of them? Or are you sorry to see them go? Your attitude will be communicated to children, even if you don't say it in words.

"Let the little children come to me," Jesus said (Matthew 19:14). If we are to grow to be like Jesus, we will be growing in kindness and love toward children.

Belonging

Everyone needs to feel that he belongs somewhere. We all need to feel that we fit in, that we are welcome. This is linked very closely to feeling significant, but it also has to do with finding a place in the group.

What are some important groups for children? Family, classmates, neighborhood friends and other friends. How do these groups make a child feel like he belongs? They include him in what they do. They encourage him to contribute to discussions. They listen and value his input. They give him a role to play that directly benefits the group, so he can see that what he does enables the group to function, even to survive.

These roles include jobs or chores. In the classroom and in families, children should have age-appropriate jobs, tasks that they can accomplish successfully. Children need to feel needed.

Exploration

Children need the freedom to explore. This does *not* mean they should be left completely to themselves, unsupervised, with no limits. It simply means they need some unstructured, nondirected free time.

Time is a precious commodity these days, and we spend much of it running here and there. We fill time with music lessons, dance lessons, gymnastics, ball practices, and games. And while those can be fun, they also can deprive a child of much-needed blocks of free time. A child needs time to think on his own, watch ants, smell clover, taste honeysuckle, blow dandelion seeds. He needs time to work through boredom and move into creativity. So children need to have access to materials that encourage them to exercise their curiosity safely, to explore and discover.

Having a variety of safe, interesting material available encourages children to explore. The adult then makes himself available as a resource person to help the child as needed. But the adult does not direct the activity or intervene in the activity unless it's necessary.

Appreciation of Childhood

Children need people who appreciate the fact that they're children. Our society pressures kids to grow up quickly. But God made children to grow and mature according to a general pattern, not only physically but mentally, emotionally, and spiritually as well. No amount of pushing and pressuring can change that.

We can manipulate kids by getting them to dress like grown-ups and talk with grown-up words, but that doesn't mean they *are* more grown up. Their appearance and speech may fool some people, but the outward signs will be out of step with the inner, God-given growth pattern. An underlying immaturity will surface.

How can we show children that we appreciate their age? How do we show that we accept them on their level? We provide activities that they can do successfully. We choose child-sized furniture and equipment for our classrooms. We make our teaching relevant to their age level and interests.

This same principle holds true for children who have special needs. We accept them as they are. If the child uses a wheelchair, we provide activities he can do successfully. If a child is color-blind, we avoid color-matching activities for him. If he is a poor reader, we avoid asking him to read the Bible passage out loud. Instead, we help these children to have accomplishments in areas where they can succeed.

Relationship

When two objects, ideas, or people are "related" to each other, that means they are linked together in some way.

"Relationship" in itself is neither positive nor negative. The link between two things could be strong or weak, good or bad. What children want and need are good, strong relationships with wise, caring adults.

In our society, generational links of relationship have broken down. God originally made the older to teach and train the younger. When the world began, and for thousands of years after that, families were intergenerational groups that worked and played together. Children were not only around parents, but grandparents, great-grandparents, aunts, and uncles. The older generations were revered for their experienced, wise counsel.

Our present-day culture centers around youth. People are separated into age-segregated peer groups. We look down our noses at the younger, and we mistrust and ridicule the older.

But children desire relationships with adults. A good, warm relationship with a caring adult can be a foundation for growth in every area of development.

The One Who Meets All Needs

Of course, only God can completely satisfy all the child's needs, so sensitive adults act as guides to lead the child to his heavenly Father, who can and will meet every need.

Security
Optimism
Significance

Belonging
Exploration
Appreciation of Childhood
Relationship

The first letters of these words spell "S.O.S. BEAR." When a child's needs have not been met, very often he will send an S.O.S. signal by his behavior. We will look specifically at behavior in a later chapter.

The adult's needs are very similar to the child's needs. Adults continue to rely on God to meet their needs too.

Praise God! He keeps us safe and secure. We can be optimistic because he is in control and is working out his plans for our good and his glory. We are significant to him, receiving our worth by the great price he paid for us. Now we belong to God the creator as precious children of the king. He has given us a whole world of interesting things and ideas to explore, as well as his rich, limitless store of wisdom and knowledge. He accepts and appreciates each of us individually right where we are in our development. And he has invited us to enter into an intimate relationship with him. He delights in our relationship. He draws us daily to fall deeper in love with him.

God's love is our greatest treasure. As we share this treasure, it multiplies like the loaves and fish. Let's continue to look for the best way to share it!

Chapter 3

The House That Faith Built

Faith Development

"When Jesus comes again,
we will all hold onto kites,
and the wind will blow and blow
and blow us up to Heaven."
—Four year old

The year Naomi was in my four-year-old class, I probably learned more from her than she learned from me. She was petite with an olive complexion, dark, straight hair, and deep brown, thoughtful eyes. She loved Jesus and was ready to share him with her friends.

In group time one night, Kara announced that her tummy hurt. Before I had time to say, "Let's pray for Kara," Naomi had already moved beside Kara. She had placed her hands on Kara's arm and was praying.

I have not seen many children who were as spiritually sensitive as Naomi. But we need not be fooled. Children are spiritual beings, just as adults are. They have deep, important questions and thoughts. They are often more ready to express a simple, matter-of-fact faith in Jesus than we adults, who have become skeptical about anything we can't experience with our five senses.

Robert Coles, in his book *The Spiritual Life of Children,* says that the research and writing of that book was "a project that, finally, helped me see children as seekers, as young pilgrims well aware that life is a finite journey and as anxious to make sense of it as those of us who are farther along in the time allotted us."[1]

The child is busy every day, working at finding his place in the world. He works at becoming his own person, finding out who he is. He works at establishing his individual identity. He works at growing up physically, mentally, emotionally, and spiritually.

We have an important role to play in helping children become all God made them to be. Our goal for children is that they become independent in their dependence on God. We want them, of their own will, to seek God and establish an eternity-long relationship with him.

Growing Up in Our Salvation

Peter wrote about wanting us to "grow up in [our] salvation" (1 Peter 2:1-3). In a sense, salvation is like the shoes or shirt I buy a size too large, knowing my son will "grow into it." We receive our salvation from Jesus. We are saved. Period. The work has been done. But salvation is much too big for us! Thanks to God's grace, we have the rest of our lives to "grow into it"!

Since we work with children, it's important to know about the growth process. It's important for us to see where children have been and where they are going. We cannot transfer our faith to them by osmosis, but we can help them "prepare him room," as the Christmas song says.

At some point, belief in the facts about Jesus must become faith in Jesus. The lifestyle of Christianity must become life in Jesus. Head knowledge must become heart knowledge. Our wills must be submitted to his will. Allegiance to "a church" and a set of doctrines must become subordinate to total surrender to Jesus. We must come to know him as our best friend, our Master, our Lord.

Some people accept Jesus' lordship earlier than others. Young children can be very sensitive to what Jesus has done for them and to how God wants them to respond. Others may not respond until they are teenagers or young adults. In either case, their response can be deep and life changing. And whether people are young or old when they come into God's kingdom, their faith continues to develop as they "grow up in salvation."

In leading people to Jesus, our place is never to manipulate them. Our job is to

- introduce them to God and his saving grace,
- feed and nurture their spirits,
- be sensitive to their readiness, and
- provide opportunities for them to express their faith as it grows, including receiving Jesus as Lord.

We must not push for what *we* would like to see happen. Instead, we must wait on God and give him room and time to work as he wills. We have the privilege of watching God work in the lives of children, so their "faith might not rest on men's wisdom, but on God's power" (1 Corinthians 2:5).

See How They Grow

In the following chapters, we'll use Erik Erikson's developmental tasks[2] to delineate stages of growth because his "tasks" have underlying spiritual significance. In each stage, we will also look at faith development as researched by James Fowler.[3] We'll look at moral development through the research of Lawrence Kohlberg[4] and Dr. William Sears.[5] And we'll see how mental development affects each stage by looking at the research of Jean Piaget[6] and Howard Gardner.[7] Of course, no researcher has complete understanding. My references to specific findings of these researchers is not meant to indicate a complete agreement with all of their theories.

Developmental stages are true in a general sense. No one is a statistic, and not everyone follows the growth pattern exactly. There is ongoing research in these areas, and other researchers may have different theories. I refer to selected, specific information from these particular sources, because the information rings true from my experience and has obvious practical applications that I find extremely helpful to me as a teacher and parent.

Growing Faith

Growing faith is a bit like building a house. We start with the foundation and then add the first floor, the second floor, and so on. All houses begin with a foundation and framework to support the walls. But the variations in house designs are infinite, from the choice of roofing and windows to paint color and flooring.

Think of some of the people of God in the Bible: Noah, Moses, David, Daniel, Mary, Peter, Paul. Each one had a deep faith in God, a faith on which their lives were founded. But they were very different individuals. They were called by God and used by him in many different ways.

The study in the following chapters shows us the structural framework for faith that is built at each stage of development. There can be a wide variation in the design of what is built around that framework. But eventually that house becomes a temple of the Holy Spirit.

One thing this study does *not* show us is the point at which head knowledge changes into a personal walk; when acceptance of a set of beliefs changes into abandoned trust in the Lord Jesus and dedication to his will. Most people who have given their lives to Jesus have done it between the ages of four and fourteen. But each person is an individual, and God graciously treats us that way.

What must a child know to come to God? What must any person believe to please God? 1) That he exists, and 2) That he rewards those who earnestly seek him. "Without faith it is impossible to please God, because anyone who comes to him must believe that he exists and that he rewards those who earnestly seek him" (Hebrews 11:6). Children are natural seekers. They just need us to point the way.

Part of our growing up in faith is based on the ongoing search to understand (the "earnest seeking" of Hebrews 11). It has helped me to realize that Abraham believed before he ever understood. God commended him for his faith, not for his understanding.

At the seaside, Jesus called to Peter and Andrew, James and John. "Follow me," he said. And they followed (Matthew 4:18-22). Jesus never asked them to understand; he just wanted them to trust.

On the hillside, Jesus told his disciples to pass five loaves and two fish to five thousand people (Matthew 14:15-21). He didn't explain it. He just asked them to trust.

On the lake, Jesus told Peter to put his fishing nets back into the water, although Peter had already fished all night long without catching anything (Luke 5:4-6). Jesus didn't expect Peter to understand. He expected Peter to trust.

As long as we live, no matter how smart we get, there will always be more of God to understand. As David said, "His greatness no one can fathom" (Psalm 145:3). So how much does a child have to understand to come to God? Not much. It's his faith that counts.

Chapter 4

A Foundation for Faith

Faith and the Infant

> From a sign posted at the church nursery door: "We will not all sleep, but we will all be changed." 1 Corinthians 15:51

According to Erikson, there is a task that corresponds to each stage of human development. In infancy, the task is to develop *trust*. If *trust* does not develop, *mistrust* is the result. Since life is a mixture of positives and negatives, there is conflict at each stage. If the positive side dominates, there emerges what Erikson called a "strength." The formation of these strengths are crucial to leading a healthy life. In the stage of infancy, when *trust* develops, the strength of *hope* emerges in the child.

What does this have to do with faith development? First of all, *trust* is a spiritual concept. God asks us to trust him. It is not easy to trust a God we can't see if we can't trust people we *can* see. Erikson himself said, "Out of the conflict between trust and mistrust, the infant develops hope which is the earliest form of what gradually becomes faith in adults."

How can we help an infant to *trust*, so that he'll develop *hope*? It's really very simple. We take care of his needs. The infant comes into the world completely dependent on others for his care. Our interaction with him communicates to him that he can trust us, or it brings about a sense of mistrust in him.

So when the infant is hungry, we feed him. When he's cold, we wrap him in a blanket. When his diaper is wet, we put a clean diaper on him. He learns that he can trust us to take care of him. When he trusts us, he has hope: hope that his needs will be met; hope that even though he is momentarily uncomfortable, everything will work out all right because there's someone taking care of him.

Now think about how this relates to basic spiritual principles. We all have needs. God meets those needs. He takes care of us. We see how God meets our needs, so we trust him. When we trust him, we have hope: hope that our needs will be met; hope that even though our situation may look bleak, everything will work out all right because there's someone taking care of us. "Now *faith* is being sure of what we *hope* for . . . " (Hebrews 11:1, italics mine).

Faith in Infancy

Paul wrote to Timothy, "From infancy you have known the holy Scriptures" (2 Timothy 3:15). Here is where faith can begin to develop. Paul refers to Timothy's mother and grandmother, who were believers before Timothy was born, so they obviously began early to guide Timothy into a trusting relationship with God.

Fowler says that infancy is a stage of "undifferentiated faith." According to Fowler, this means that the beginnings of trust, courage, hope, and love are mixed together into one feeling: good. They are not experienced as separate feelings. In simple terms, the infant begins to feel a very basic sense of good and bad, pain and pleasure. I call it the stage of "seed faith."

Fowler also says, "The strength of trust, autonomy, hope

and courage (or their opposites) developed in this phase underlie (or threaten to undermine) all that comes later in the faith development." Are you important if you teach infants? Yes! Can you as a parent or teacher help infants learn anything spiritually significant? Yes! You can help them to trust.

We introduce babies to God in very simple ways. First, we point out God's creation. When the infant eats a banana, we say, "God made the banana." When he smells a flower, we say, "God made the flower." When he feels the rain sprinkle down on him, we say, "God made the rain." At first, the infant does not know the word *God*, but he sees, smells, touches, tastes, and hears the world God made. So we begin to make the connection for him. We are introducing him to God.

We do a similar thing in order to teach about God's care and love. When the infant is cold, we wrap a warm blanket around him or we put a sweater on him. We say, "I'm taking care of you. God takes care of you." When we are rocking the infant in a peaceful moment, we say, "I love you. God loves you." The infant does not know the words *God* or *care* or *love*. But he does know the feeling he's having at those moments, the feeling of being loved and cared for. So we begin to make the connection for him. We are introducing him to God.

What's Going on in the Infant's Mind?

Since we are created in God's image, we are born with intellect. We've been made with certain built-in capabilities like creativity, exploration and discovery, the drive to communicate, laughter, personality, and temperament. Researchers who don't believe in God are still trying to determine how these can be present in babies.

An infant is not a completely blank slate when he's born, but he has a lot to learn. Where is he in mental ability? How does his mind develop?

An infant's world is very tangible. It consists of what he sees, hears, smells, touches, and tastes. Everything is new. Everything is being discovered. Piaget labeled this time a "sensorimotor" stage. That means infants are using their senses to learn about the world around them. Their motor skills are also developing and infants use these skills to help them discover.

But there are other ways in which the infant is learning. Infants are fascinated by faces. This is one clue that points to the fact that infants want interaction with other people. In these interactions, their communication skills grow.

An infant's learning is also affected by his personality and temperament. His culture affects how he learns. And he is born into a specific, unique family situation that will affect his learning.

Developing Morality

According to Lawrence Kohlberg, the infant is in a premoral position. He does not yet have a perspective of self and others. A child is born completely egocentric. The world revolves around him. Even Mom and Dad are an extension of himself.

The infant is, of course, born with a tendency to sin. He is aware of feeling good and bad, pain and pleasure. He knows the difference between the smiles and frowns he sees. He soon learns "yes" and "no," as well as the tone of voice and body language that indicates something is good or bad.

The infant depends on these outward cues to tell him what's right and wrong. He does not yet discriminate between right and wrong on his own. He is being trained.

The Challenge

I often ask people who attend my faith development seminar what an infant is like. What do they enjoy? What do they do? Parents, grandparents, and teachers who have infants raise their hands. "They like to hear singing." "They like to put things in their mouths." "They like to watch faces." "They like to be held." These people are the experts on infants. They know what an infant likes.

If you are around an infant, you can do on a small scale what researchers do. Watch and listen. Find out what motivates the infant you work with. What does he like?

Now you have a challenge. You know what the infant does. You know what he likes. How can you communicate God to the infant through the things he does and likes? How can you make God *relevant* to his life? This is your challenge. But it's one you can meet, and you will be greatly rewarded for it.

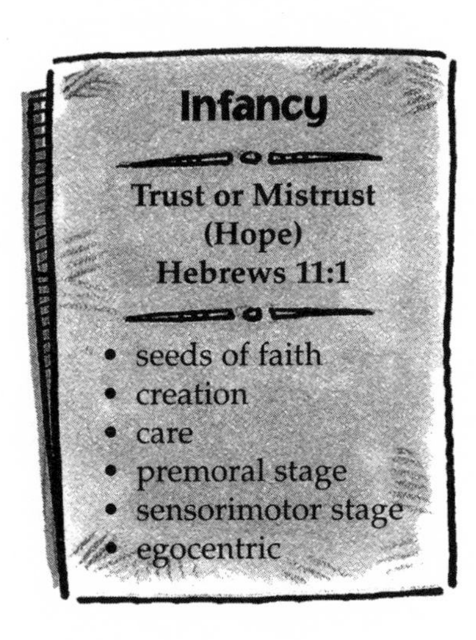

Chapter 5

The "Me" Stage

Faith in Early Childhood

"Does God have a paci (pacifier)?"
—Two year old

Early childhood, in this growth study, includes children two and three years old. Erikson says that the child this age develops either *autonomy* or *shame*. An autonomous person is a person who rules himself. This is just what two and three year olds seem to want. They are beginning the process of becoming independent from Mom and Dad. They are becoming their own persons.

Two and three year olds want to do things for themselves. To help a child this age develop a sense of autonomy, adults can look for things the child can do for himself. Show him what he can do. He can learn to brush his teeth, wash his face, pick up his toys, put on Velcro-fastened shoes, and many other things. As he learns to be independent in these small ways, he feels a sense of *autonomy*.

Of course, there are many things that a young child is not capable of doing and there are many things he is not allowed to do. The key is the attitude of the adult. Encourage the child. If he needs help, step in to help him without criticizing and judging. Instead, express your confidence in his abilities. Show how proud you are that he's getting bigger and will one day be doing these things by himself.

If the child is not allowed to begin doing things for himself, or if he's constantly criticized and put down, he will develop a sense of shame. Erikson says shame is a feeling of being exposed. In this case, the child feels that what has been exposed is his own deficiency and inadequacy.

When the child moves through this stage feeling a sense of *autonomy*, then the strength of *will* develops. Twos and threes are often called "strong-willed" children. This is actually a good thing. God has planned for all of us to develop our own wills. He gives us free will. Then he asks us to choose to submit our wills to his. David wrote, "Teach me to do your will, for you are my God" (Psalm 143:10).

Faith in Early Childhood

Fowler tells us that children are now forming their ideas and images of what God is like. They often think of him with very human characteristics.

I call this the "fantasy/imitative" stage, based on how Fowler describes this stage of faith development. He says this is "the fantasy-filled, imitative phase in which the child can be powerfully and permanently influenced by examples, moods, actions and stories" of the significant adults in his life. This stage of faith lasts until the child is about six or seven.

Imagination plays a big part in the lives of young children, who have difficulty distinguishing between fantasy and reality, as we learned earlier. The made-up stories of TV superheroes and the real-life stories of Jesus' miracles may be given the same importance in the child's mind. It's good for us to point out what's real and what's not. But it's also important for us not to be surprised if young children still confuse the two.

Fowler emphasizes the adult's tremendous responsibility at this stage. He says, "The imagination and fantasy life of a child can be exploited by witting or unwitting adults." The religious stories, images, and symbols we share with children "can prove life-opening and sustaining of love, faith and courage," or they can give rise "to fear, rigidity and the brutalization of souls." Young children generally believe what they are told without questioning whether it is true.

The "imitative" label on this stage is important. Young children will imitate the significant adults around them. They cannot enter the adult's world, but they can imitate it. So the outward evidences of an adult's faith may be imitated by a young child. He may play church or pretend to pray or baptize a stuffed animal.

Some time should be spent here thinking about the term *significant adult*. The question might be asked, "Who are the significant adults in the child's life?" The obvious, traditional answer is "Mom and Dad," but this is not always the case. It's true that parents will always have a significant impact on their children, even if one or both parents are gone. The absence of a parent is indeed significant. However, the term *significant adult* means an adult whose influence on the child affects the child's choices.

To find out who are the significant people in a child's life, ask, "Who spends time with the child—not just in the same house, but *with* the child? Who listens to the child? Who plays with the child?" The answers to these questions will usually reveal the identity of the significant people in the child's life, and they may not always be adults.

What's Going on in the Young Child's Mind?

The child has by now learned to use words to communicate, but he understands many more words than he uses in his speech. His perspective is still egocentric; he sees the world only from his viewpoint.

Piaget called this the "preoperational" stage, which begins around age two and lasts until about age seven. *Operation* is a word Piaget used to describe a thought process that allows a child "to do in his mind what before was done physically." It describes logical reasoning. *Preoperational* means that this stage of development comes before a child can reason logically. As we saw in chapter 1, the young child operates by his own logic and is not capable of reasoning like adults do. He thinks differently.

Twos and threes like predictable schedules and routines. This gives them a sense of security. But they are also very curious. They are now aware of more of the outside world that revolves around their everyday activities, and they move through their world like a whirlwind. They want to find out how they affect the world. They perform simple cause-and-effect experiments: What will happen if I push this button, pull this string, or take that apart? All this exploring keeps the adults around them hopping.

Developing Morality

According to Kohlberg, young children look to external clues to tell them whether something is right or wrong. They ask whether the action would be punished or rewarded. So rules, consistently enforced, help train them to know what's right and what's wrong.

In fact, rules help young children feel safe and secure. They sense their own difficulty in controlling themselves, so when there is a trustworthy person around to do the controlling, they don't have to be afraid of what might happen. They feel protected.

Toddlers may have to be told the same rule over and over again. They have a hard time making that rule a part of their thinking. They are just emerging from a completely egocentric stage. Everything they see, smell, taste, touch, or hear is "mine." However, at about eighteen months, they begin to get a glimmer of understanding that other people have feelings and needs too. But throughout the early childhood stage, they still have a difficult time telling the difference between "mine" and "yours." They engage in what's called "parallel play." That means they play side by side, but they are not playing together.

The Challenge

Do you know any two and three year olds? What do they like to do? What do they talk about? What do they like to play with? What do they like to see, hear, taste, smell, and touch? What are they "into"? What games do they like to play? You can become the expert by watching and listening to them. Add your own observations to what you have just learned in this chapter.

Now that you know all of this, your challenge is to answer the question, "How do I communicate God to two and three year olds, using their interests? How can I make God's Word relevant to the young child?"

Chapter 6

The Discoverers

The Faith of Fours and Fives

"Teacher! I'm five and nine quarters!"
—Five year old

At this stage, children develop either *initiative* or *guilt*. A person with initiative does things without being asked. He takes the offensive. He thinks independently. He's what we would call a self-starter. This describes children who are four and five years old. They are little scientists. They are seeing more and more of the world around them, and they have lots of questions about it. They set out to explore, examine, and discover everything. They want to learn and know.

When a child is encouraged to follow his natural inclination to explore and find out, he develops a sense of *initiative*. There are, of course, limits to what the four- or five-year-old child is capable of doing. There are also things that he will not be allowed to explore. But when he is ridiculed or put down, or when he is continually restricted and told he is not capable, he begins to feel *guilt*.

It's not that adults should let the child do anything he wants. But adults should have an encouraging attitude toward the child's God-given desire for knowledge and his attempts at exploration. There are encouraging ways of saying no. For example, "I'm glad you want to know about that, but now is not the time. We'll plan another time when you can do that." Sometimes simply substituting an acceptable avenue of exploration for an unacceptable one solves the problem.

One area in which the curious child can easily swamp adults is with his questions. Young children ask hundreds of questions every day. Some of these questions are quite deep. When one of my sons was five, he asked, "Why does the skin on your body never end?" Other questions are so off-the-wall that they have no real, logical answers.

Frustrated adults sometimes respond, "That's a silly question!" "Where did you come up with a question like that?" "I've had it with all these questions!" "I don't want to hear another question!" Responses like these cause the child to feel guilt. He doesn't know it's natural for him to ask questions. As far as he knows, he may be the only person in the world who's dumb enough not to know the answer.

There are some encouraging, initiative-promoting responses that are easy for adults to make. A good start is, "That's a good question!" It's always all right to say, "I don't know." It's even better to say, "What do you think?" Then the child can give his opinion. This helps him feel that his ideas and thoughts are valuable.

Sometimes the answer to a question is a matter of research, but the question comes at a time when it's not possible to look up the answer. Then a good response is, "We'll try to find out after lunch." Or, "We'll try to find a book about that at the library." This not only values his question, but it helps him learn how to learn.

When a child develops his sense of *initiative* during this stage, the strength of *purpose* emerges. The child feels, "There's a purpose for my curiosity. There's a purpose for me and my questions. There's a purpose for me in God's world." David felt the strength of purpose. He wrote, "The Lord will fulfill his purpose for me" (Psalm 138:8).

Faith in Four and Five Year Olds

The four and five year olds are still in the fantasy/imitative stage of faith that began around age two. They are living what they imagine, and they are imitating the visible faith of significant adults. For a more thorough review of this stage, see the Faith section in the last chapter. The child's understandings are intuitive. He feels and understands without rational thought, although as he grows, his ability to reason also grows.

What's Going on in the Minds of Fours and Fives?

Fours and fives are still in what Piaget called the preoperational stage. But some significant mental skills are developing. Howard Gardner says that one of the most important skills that develops is the ability to understand and work with symbols. As the child grows from age two to around age six or seven, this ability increases. He is growing from literal interpretations to understanding the symbolic. And by five, he's beginning to see the difference between fantasy and reality.

Fours and fives begin to realize that they are growing. They will not be babies forever. So they are very proud of their age. In fact, some of them may announce how old they are every time they come to class. This motivates other children to chime in and tell how old *they* are. Growing is a new concept to them: getting older, better, smarter, and stronger.

This interest in age may also have to do with the fact that they are now a great deal more interested in numbers and counting. In fact, Howard Gardner has called this an important "wave" in their growing ability to make and use symbols. Four year olds seem to want to count everything.

Because exploration and discovery are so much a part of

their lives, the fours and fives begin seeing a lot more of what's happening in the world around them. There's a lot they don't understand, so they may develop fears they've not had before. They want and need understanding and comfort.

The four year old is becoming less egocentric. Before this time, he played beside other children, but their playing was not real cooperation. Now he begins what is called "associative play." This means he starts interacting with other children when he plays. "You be the mommy and I'll be the baby," he'll say. "You be the store man and I'll come and buy some food." Or, "You make the road with the blocks and I'll drive my car over it."

Developing Morality

Fours and fives still depend on rules (and the enforcement of those rules) to guide them in knowing and choosing what's right and what's wrong. However, their conscience is beginning to develop. The teaching and training of the earlier years is beginning to be internalized. Now they don't have to be told as often. They know that it's wrong to take toys from other children. It's right to share. It's wrong to hit. It's right to help. Of course, they will not always go by what their developing conscience tells them. They need external help to confirm when they are on the right or wrong track.

Fours and fives are starting to understand the concept of consequences, cause and effect, if/then. They share selectively: they pick and choose what to share and when. They still have trouble seeing from any viewpoint but their own.

The Challenge

Do you know four- and five-year-old children? What are they "into"? What do they like and dislike? What do they enjoy doing, hearing, seeing, smelling, and tasting? What games do they like to play? What do they talk about? Add your answers to the information you've learned in this chapter. Now your challenge is to decide how to communicate God and his Word to fours and fives through what they enjoy. Make it relevant to their lives. This is where you will be most successful.

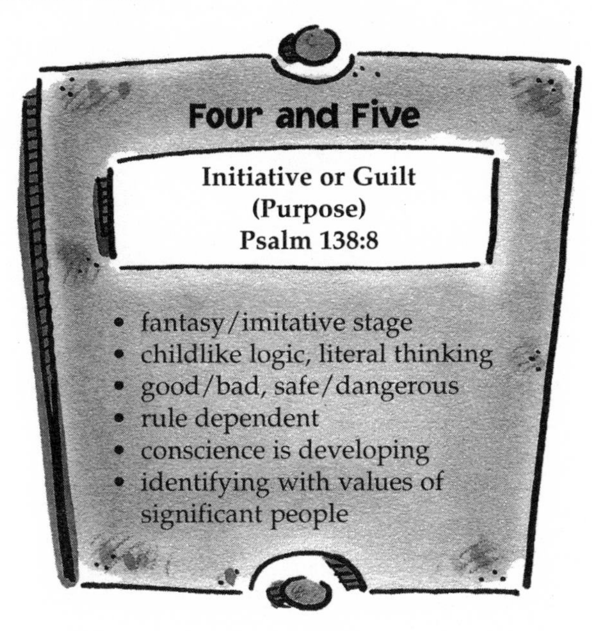

Now the most important character-shaping and faith-shaping years are almost over. Francis Xavier, a Jesuit leader, said, "Give me the children until they are seven, and anyone may have them afterwards."[1] The preschool years are perhaps the most important years of a person's life. Although major changes can and do happen later, by age six or seven basic foundations have been laid within the child that will underlie the rest of his life. David Kherdian, in *The Road From Home,* wrote, "What you learn in old age is carved on ice. What you learn in childhood is carved on stone."[2]

Chapter 7

A Bigger World

The "School" Years

"Sometimes we say, 'I'm not playing with you ever again!' But me and you say that all the time, but come back in about an hour and say, 'Sorry.' Besides, friends are friends, and friends we'll be forever."

—Eight year old

The elementary stage covers ages six through eleven. A lot of development occurs during those years. There's a great deal of difference between the six year old and the nine year old. There's a great deal of difference between the nine year old and the eleven year old. But Erikson looked at this span of years and saw that children at these ages had something in common. He said these years were critical in creating either a sense of *industry* or a sense of *inferiority* in the growing child.

An industrious person is someone who is busy doing productive things. That typifies the elementary child. He wants to use his developing physical skills. He wants to see how fast he can run and how high he can jump. He wants to make and build things. He wants to be useful. When he is encouraged in his efforts to be busy and productive, he develops a sense of *industry*.

But *inferiority* is the negative side of this stage. The child can develop a sense of inferiority if the adults in his life set the goals too high and he cannot live up to their expectations. This is especially true if the child perceives that love and acceptance is conditional, based on his performance and achievement. For him, the consequences of failure are enormous.

Inferiority can also develop if the adult does the work for the child. Adults know they can do projects faster and better, but when the adult takes over, the child gets the feeling that the adult thinks he is not capable. His work is not good enough.

Inferiority can develop if a child is not allowed to practice his skills. Every time he gets out the glue and paint, he is told to put them away, "Don't get all that stuff out again. You know all you'll do is just make a big mess." It may not be the right time to "pull the stuff out," but the key to saying no is to say it in an encouraging way. "I'm so glad you're interested in building. There will be some time Saturday afternoon when you can build all you want."

When a child goes through this stage developing the positive sense of *industry*, he reaps the bonus of gaining a strength: *competence*. He feels competent. He is capable. He can do it. This very powerful strength is the basis for many accomplishments that lie ahead. Then as the years go on and he develops in faith, he will come to the place of realizing that it was God who energized him to accomplish so much. The apostle Paul was quite competent. But he said, "Our competence comes from God" (2 Corinthians 3:5).

Faith in the Elementary Years

Competence breeds confidence. Confidence helps the child stand strong in his faith. It helps him share his faith with others. But what is his faith like at this stage?

This is the "story-centered" stage of faith because "story" plays such a big role. According to Fowler, "the person begins to take on for himself the stories, beliefs and observances that symbolize belonging to his or her community." Also, the child is beginning to be able to tell his own stories of faith.

What kind of stories affect a child's faith? The very obvious stories are the Bible stories that they read and hear. They are particularly interested in the mighty men and women of God and how God worked in their lives. We communicate the Bible stories to children most effectively by making them real and relevant.

But there are other kinds of stories that affect the faith of children. These are the random stories they hear from us. We tell stories all the time, although we may not realize it. Whenever we see a friend in the parking lot at the mall, we may stand around and talk. "We just got back from vacation, and you'll never guess who I saw at church. I hadn't seen them in ages, and . . . and . . . and . . . " We are telling a story. The same thing happens when the phone rings and we begin to visit with the person who has called us. The same thing happens at church when we stand around and visit afterward. We are telling our stories.

Children are listening. They stand there waiting for us. Or they listen from another room. Or they hear us as they pass us in the hall at church. And they are affected by what they hear. They are affected by our stories.

To take advantage of this, we can begin telling children how God has worked and is working in our lives. We can invite other adults to tell their stories in our classrooms. These might be missionaries who are visiting or someone who has come to God out of a life of drugs or atheism.

Then we can begin asking children to tell *their* stories. Fowler points out that this stage is a time when children have the ability to tell their own experiences. They can tell what God is doing in their lives. Together, their stories, your stories, and Bible stories are strong faith builders.

During this time, children talk about church as if it were their club.[1] "My church does it this way. Jonathan's church does it that way. Here's what they do at Megan's church." It's not bad for a child to feel about church the way that he would feel about a club because there's something very important that a club gives its members: a sense of belonging. We want the children who come to our churches to feel like they belong. They are valued members.

Children in the elementary years are also beginning to sense their need for God. They are seeing more of the world around them. Most of them are now out in the community in schools and on teams. Their relationships now encompass other people from varied backgrounds. They experience the ups and downs of friendship and being accepted by the group. And, sadly enough, many of them experience the difficulties of their parents' problems at home that are "resolved" by divorce or separation.

In the years before, Mom and Dad could solve any problem. But now children begin to see that there are problems even Mom and Dad can't solve. All of this adds up to a strong sense of the need for a faithful friend—a strong protector, always available, wise enough to solve any problem—God. Perhaps this is why many children accept Jesus as Lord during this time. They know they need him.

What's Going on in the Elementary Mind?

According to Piaget, the six year old is moving out of the preoperational stage—unable to reason and think logically—and into the "concrete operational" stage. Piaget says that this stage lasts through age eleven. The child is able to reason logically about things that are concrete, not abstract. In other words, he has to see or handle something. It must be physically present for him to reason logically about it.

Recent research has shown that in some areas, children reach the concrete operational stage earlier than seven.

Howard Gardner says that a child may be preoperational in the area of language, but concrete operational in the area of drawing or number.[2] This would account for some children who seem to understand symbolism in certain areas much earlier than others.

However, age seven is often known as the "age of reason." By then the child has moved from literal interpretations of words, events, and stories to an understanding of symbolism and deeper meanings.

By the age of eight, he's able to perceive distance and space accurately. He has an understanding of the flow of time. When he was younger, "long ago" meant yesterday. But now, "long ago" means the distant past. He begins to study events of history and can perceive them chronologically.

By age nine, he's at what some have called "the golden age of memory." He's able to retain lots of information. Many children seem to be able to memorize easily at this time.

At ten, he's easygoing. He's interested in trying a variety of experiences. He begins to be interested in what's going on in other people's minds. What do they think?

Then somewhere between the ages of ten and eleven, something happens. The boys start becoming more restless. The girls become moody. They can concentrate longer, but they become critical of adults. The door to the child's bedroom, which was always open before, is now closed. A sign may be posted on it: Do Not Enter. Communication decreases. They are about to enter the next stage: adolescence.

Developing Morality

Between the ages of seven and ten, children develop the ability to tell whether something is true or false, right or wrong. But they still depend on rules to guide their behavior.

Children at this stage are very alert to infractions of the rules. When a rule has been broken, they are quick to point it out. They are sensitive to justice. "It's not fair" is a common complaint. They have an "eye for an eye, tooth for a tooth" sense of morality.

The Challenge

Do you know children who are in their elementary years? What are they "into"? What do they like to do? What do they enjoy? What music do they like to listen to? What games do they like to play? What do they talk about? Add your answers to the information you may have learned in this chapter. Now your challenge is to communicate God and his Word through what these children are "into," through what they enjoy. How can you make God and his Word relevant to their world?

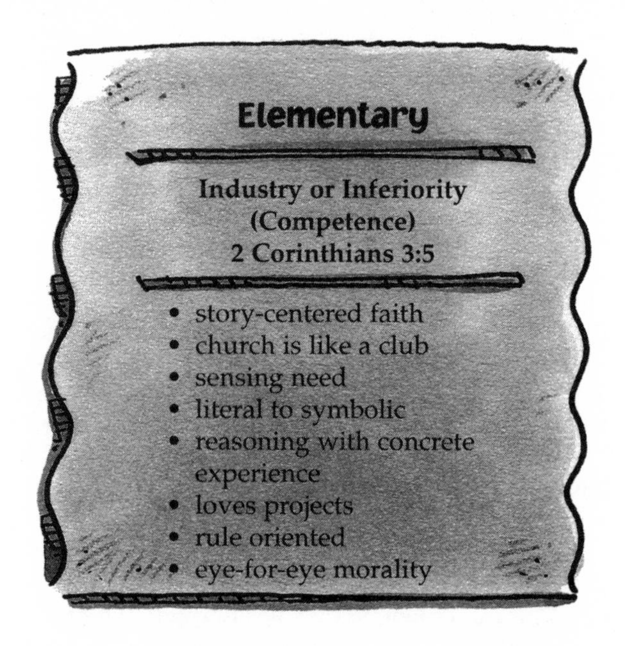

Chapter 8

Pulling Away

Faith in Adolescence

A parent commented to his fourteen year old that math these days was much easier because kids can use calculators to solve the problems.

His son responded, "Easier? No way. Math is hard. You have to learn which buttons to push."

Ages twelve through nineteen are the teenage years, or adolescence. Kids in this age bracket are not children anymore. They are young adults. They are beginning the last stage of what began in infancy: becoming an independent individual.

The main task of an adolescent is to develop a sense of *identity*. This means that he must figure out who he is, what he believes, and where he plans to go. He must explore the different roles that are available to him, and he must choose a path to pursue for the future.

One way parents and teachers can encourage teens to develop their sense of identity is to listen to them. Let them question. Teens often try ideas on for size and sometimes they express themselves very strongly in certain areas just to hear themselves take a stand.

Another way to encourage teens to develop identity is to

let them make more and more of their own decisions as they move through the teen years. Let them make some mistakes while it's safe and they can have adult support.

If the teen is still treated like he's a ten year old, if his views and opinions are not valued and listened to, or if someone maps out all his future paths for him, he will develop a sense of *identity confusion*.

When the teen is developing his own identity, then the strength of *fidelity* becomes his. Fidelity is faithfulness. When the young person knows who he is, he can be faithful to his beliefs and values. Isaiah talked to King Ahaz about fidelity. He said, "If you do not stand firm in your faith, you will not stand at all" (Isaiah 7:9).

Faith in Adolescence

Adolescence is a time of "personalizing faith." The teen is involved in and affected by many arenas of life, including family, school, peers, work, the media, his church group, hobbies, and other interests. Fowler says that the young person has to understand how his faith relates to all these involvements. His faith must be personal. The teen wants to know God as someone who knows and accepts him. His faith "must provide a basis for identity and outlook."

Ultimately, no arena in which the young person is involved will fulfill him. There will be disappointments and difficulties in every area. Kevin Huggins, a professor of counseling, talks about this in his book, *Parenting Adolescents*. He writes, "One of the most important developmental tasks an adolescent has to accomplish [is] to come to the realization that his deepest desires cannot be met anywhere except in a relationship with Christ."[1]

So during this stage, there will be questions and tension. But this leads the teen toward personalizing faith, making it his own. He is not imitating his parents' faith. He is not just doing what is popular among his youth group. He is developing a strong relationship with Jesus on his own. These are *his* beliefs, *his* values, *his* faith.

A Christian's identity is found in who he is in Jesus. Paul wrote, "We, who with unveiled faces all reflect the Lord's glory, are being transformed into his likeness with ever-increasing glory, which comes from the Lord, who is the Spirit" (2 Corinthians 3:18). Part of reflecting his glory is revealing who we are by revealing who he is. It's Christ in us. He becomes the source and essence of our identity as we grow up in faith. So this is where the teen is headed.

What's Going on in the Adolescent's Mind?

By now, the adolescent has entered into the "formal operational" stage, according to Piaget. He is beginning to reason logically. He begins to see many options open to him. This may make decision-making difficult. He can think about abstract concepts and hypothetical situations. He can think about thinking. As this stage progresses, his thinking becomes more like an adult's. He is maturing.

However, Kevin Huggins reports that many teens today choose not to use formal thinking. Why? Maybe because of stress. Maybe because formal thinking often grows through pain and problems, and these are things we try to avoid. Maybe because the best way to develop mature thinking is to interact with other people who are thinking maturely.[2] Many young people spend most of their time associating with their peers and very little time associating with mature adults.

Developing Morality

Since a teen sees many options, he may contemplate how different value systems would work in his life. He's looking for what "fits" him. He also starts thinking about what's good for society.

Because the teen's mind can now reason formally, he can think about how others must be thinking about him. He becomes very conscious of other people's opinions, particularly their opinions about him.

One of the teen's strong desires is to be accepted, so his morality tends to become a "conformist morality." When he has a decision to make between right and wrong, he will ask, "What will *they* think of me if I do this (or if I don't do this)?" The *they* in question are the people who are significant to him. *They* might be his school peer group, or his church youth group, or his youth director or teacher, or his parents. But whoever they are, they will play a strong role in influencing his decisions about morality.

The Challenge

Do you know any teenagers? What do they like? What are they "into"? What do they enjoy doing? What kind of music do they like? What kinds of games do they play? What do they talk about? They have a variety of personalities and a variety of likes and dislikes. Is there a common ground?

Look at your answers to these questions. Add that to the information you may have learned in this chapter. Now your challenge is to communicate God and his Word to teens through what they enjoy. How can you communicate in ways they can understand? How can you make God and his Word relevant to their world?

What If . . . ?

As the child grows into and through adulthood, he continues to go through developmental stages. According to Erikson, after the teen years, the young adult goes through a transi-

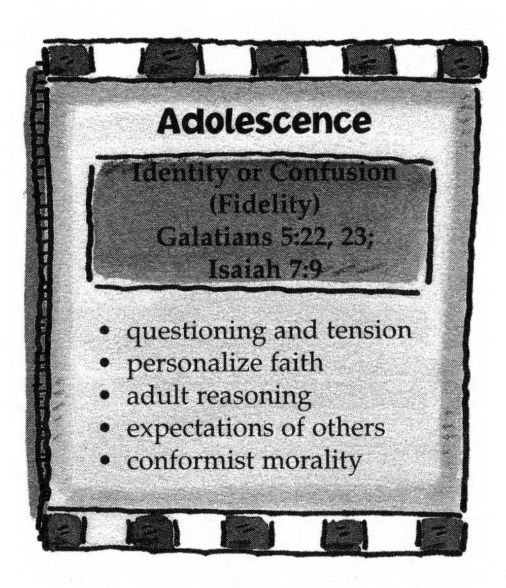

tional period, during which he develops a strong, intimate friendship with a best friend or he develops a sense of isolation. Then he goes through middle adulthood busily "generating"—working, producing, providing—or else stagnating. The last stage is older adulthood, during which he feels a sense of integrity or a sense of despair.

Now a question comes up: What if a person didn't develop a sense of trust in infancy? What if he didn't develop a sense of industry and competence in his school years? Does he get stuck at that stage?

The answer is no. A person progresses through all the stages. We can compare it again to building a house. All the floors will be added on, one by one. But if there's a crack in the foundation, that may cause problems in the house later on. If the negative side of a stage develops instead of the positive side, the person will move on, carrying with him the negative sense that he received from that stage. As an adult, he may have an underlying sense of shame or undue guilt. He may feel inferior. Or he may not have a strong sense of identity.

Then what can we do if someone has developed the negative side instead of the positive? There is hope. First of all, children are very resilient. They bounce back and usually forgive easily. Just because there's a crack somewhere doesn't mean the house will fall down.

Second, God is in control. None of us is perfect, and as we work with children at home or in the classroom, we need to pray, "Father, make up for my deficiencies as a parent or teacher." In Joel 2:25, God promises his people, "I will repay you for the years the locusts have eaten." God can patch the cracks.

Third, there are things that can be done to help repair the damage. Christian counselors can help when the damage is severe, when the pain of the past has a stranglehold on the present or the future. But there are ways others can help as well.

Perhaps you are working in class with a child who is having problems. You suspect that he never developed a sense of trust. Then in your relationship with him, you can show him that you are trustworthy. Your love and respect for him are unconditional. Whether a person missed out on trust or autonomy or initiative or industry or identity, your role is the same. Accept and encourage him by giving him doses of the positive input he missed at that earlier stage in life. Pray for him, and show him how Jesus can meet his needs.

*following Erik Erikson's tasks and strengths

Communication in the CLASSROOM

Chapter 9

From the Heart the Mouth Speaks

Communicating With Children

Child: Why don't we pray for the West Coast?
Mom: We do, sweetheart. We pray for the whole world.
Child: But at church, we say, "In the name of the Father, the Son, and the whole East Coast."

Peter Smith, a specialist in children's literature and learning skills, tells about the time he took his preschool daughter to a dairy farm. She watched intently as the cows were milked by the milking machines. Mr. Smith was very pleased that his daughter would have a head start when she got to school, having learned about the farm.

But a few weeks later, Mr. Smith found that his daughter hadn't quite understood. He was remembering the dairy farm with his daughter, when she commented, "Those cows sure drink a lot of milk." She had thought the milk was going into the cows instead of coming out.

Try reading the dialogue on the next page. If you have trouble, read it aloud slowly.

M R DUCKS.
M R KNOT.
O S A R.
C M WANGS?
L I B, M R DUCKS.

M R SNAKES.
M R KNOT.
O S A R.
C M B D I'S?
L I B, M R SNAKES.

M R FARMERS.
M R KNOT.
O S A R.
C M M T POCKETS?
L I B, M R FARMERS.

M R MICE.
M R KNOT.
O S A R.
C M E D B D FEET?
L I B, M R MICE.

Did you figure it out? Do U C? Sometimes children have a hard time figuring out what we are trying to say.

Try this. The next time you are with the children you teach, play this popular game. I'm sure you remember it from your childhood. It's called:

A singularity, solanium tuberosum,
A duplication, solanium tuberosum,
A triumvirate, solanium tuberosum,
A quaternity.

I'm sure you remember how to play it. Everybody used to play it. Of course, you may remember it as "One potato, two potato, three potato, four."

Sometimes we sound as confusing as Latin to children when we try to communicate in ways that they don't understand. Is there anything we can do to make sure we communicate well?

Nonverbal Communication

Misunderstandings will occasionally occur, even when we're communicating to other adults. But there are some things we can do to increase our chances of being understood.

First of all, we must realize that most of our communication is done without words. We communicate through our tone of voice. Try saying "I love you" in a sarcastic tone of voice. What will that communicate to the listener? We believe tone of voice more than the words that are spoken.

Another factor in communication is body language. Tightly folded arms indicate a protective, impatient, or defensive attitude. Droopy shoulders communicate discouragement. When communicating with a child, good body language includes getting on the child's level so you can literally see "eye to eye." A gentle, friendly pat on the arm or shoulder can also help.

Then there are facial expressions. A smile is warm and welcoming. Tightly closed lips and clenched teeth indicate anger.

A UCLA researcher, Albert Mehrabian, did a study to see just how important these nonverbal cues are in our communication. He found out that fifty-five percent of our communication comes from what people see when we talk to them—our body language, gestures, and even our appearance. Our tone of voice communicates thirty-eight percent of what they hear. Only seven percent of what we communicate comes through our actual words, the content of what we are saying.[1]

Stop, Look, and Listen

We have already looked at one of the important factors in communication: being aware of "where" the children are mentally, morally, and spiritually. We are like missionaries. It's like going into another culture. We have to learn to speak the language. We have to try see the world through their eyes. We must also listen.

For several years, I taught writing classes for upper elementary grades, junior high, and high school. For one assignment, fifth graders wrote a paper entitled "What Am I?" Some of the papers were very revealing. One girl wrote, "What am I? A best friend to some, an enemy to others, a little voice coming from behind the wall that no one hears."

Another girl wrote, "What am I? I am the little girl in the ballerina suit twirling and spinning around and around. The little girl who got up on stage and sang a song at preschool graduation. The little girl with food on her face. I am the little girl walking just in a diaper. I am also the little schoolgirl doing her homework. I am just a painting on the wall that nobody hardly looks at."

Children know when no one is listening. And children's feelings are no different than ours. When somebody listens to us, we feel valued.

But it's not only the children who benefit when an adult listens to them. The adult benefits too. Among other insights the adult might gain are insights into the child's needs. And we have to know what the needs are if we're going to minister to those needs.

I taught four year olds at church for many years. At the beginning of one year, there was a little boy who was particularly rambunctious. Jonathan couldn't seem to keep his hands off the other children. It was hard for him to focus on the learning activities.

I was the supervising teacher, so when the children went to different learning activity centers, I went from center to center, making sure everything was all right. I would watch and listen and help wherever I was needed. I happened to be with Jonathan's group one day when they were drawing pictures. I thought I had heard Jonathan say that he was drawing a picture of a cougar.

I knelt beside him and watched. His lips were set tightly together. His eyes were focused intently on the paper. He gripped the crayon in his hand and drew big circles on the paper, around and around and around.

I said, "Jonathan, I like the colors you're using to make your cougar."

"It's not a cougar," Jonathan said. He kept making circles, gazing at his paper. "It's a big, fat female."

I was so surprised, I wanted to laugh. But I didn't. (One rule of communication: Don't laugh at what kids say unless they are trying to tell a joke. They may be absolutely serious.)

I didn't say anything, probably more because I couldn't think of what to say than because I thought this was an important listening moment. But I just kept watching and listening. Then Jonathan said something that opened a big door of understanding.

He was still drawing circles furiously. Without looking up, he said, "My mommy and my daddy is makin' problems, and my daddy is gonna move out."

All of a sudden, I knew why Jonathan behaved the way he did in class. He was angry and confused and lost. He didn't know how to handle his feelings.

Listening is so important. It helps us know where kids are mentally, morally, spiritually, and emotionally.

Robert Coles, author of *The Spiritual Life of Children*, was asked in an interview, "Do you think we miss out on opportunities to know children by failing to listen to them?"

He answered, "Yes, I do. Remember, Jesus said that the children in some way will be a clue to eternity. Children were not meant to be put in the straitjackets that some of us want them to be in, to hold their breath until they grow up. They offer us a chance to see a good part of what we are: human beings struggling to figure out what this world means. They ask all sorts of wonderful questions in that regard."[2]

How can we learn to communicate better? We can stop, look, and listen.

Play

Dr. Robert Hemfelt, a psychologist, and Dr. Paul Warren, a behavioral pediatrician, have coauthored several books about parent-child relationships. They say that "play is the single most effective way to communicate with children less than nine years old."[3] Why? Play provides a comfortable format for communication.

Kelly Bates works at Vanderbilt Hospital in Nashville,

Tennessee. Her job is to help children who've come to the hospital to undergo a traumatic type of treatment or who have already been through a trauma. She was once asked, "How do you get children to trust you? They don't know you, and you are only with them for a short time."

"I play with them," she said.

When you play with children, you can talk with each other. You get to know each other. They grow to trust you. And you are communicating to them that they are so important to you that you will give them one of your most precious possessions: time.

This is true not only for young children, but for preteens and teens as well. My husband and I have experienced this in our own family. We have two teenage sons. Some of our best times of conversation are when we play cards together, or when we play badminton, or when we put on the ball gloves and go outside to play catch. Working together and playing together: these are times of communication.

How does this translate to the classroom? We should not be afraid to enjoy activities. We should not be afraid to play because that's the best way to communicate.

Give Positive Instructions

Children often hear, "Don't do this. Don't do that." Life is full of "don'ts." But we can often say the same things in a positive way.

I was once demonstrating teaching techniques to a group of parents. As I handed paper cups to the children, I said, "Keep the cups in a cup shape." The parents laughed at me. It did sound funny. I could have said, "Don't crush the cups." Instead, I was deliberately trying to be positive. Sometimes this results in some very creative sentences!

There are advantages to being positive, besides just encouraging positive thinking. First of all, if I had said, "Don't crush the cups," I would have given that idea to several children who hadn't thought of it yet. Second, by being positive, I limited their alternatives.

For example, if I want my class to walk down the hall quietly, I don't tell them, "Don't run." Why? Because that would leave them many other options. They could skip, roll, dance, jump, and find lots of other creative ways to get down the hall. And they are still obeying me, aren't they? They are not running. But if I say, "Walk quietly," I have given them only one option: my choice.

In one of the Laura Ingalls Wilder's books, Laura and her sister Mary spend a day sliding down the straw stack. When Pa comes home, he is upset because the straw is now scattered across the yard. He has to restack it. He says, "You girls mustn't slide down the straw stack any more."

After dinner, Laura and Mary take a walk outside. They walk close to the straw stack and begin sniffing the straw. Soon Laura is rolling in the straw. "Come on, Mary!" she calls. "Pa didn't say we can't roll!"

Pa is angry until he sees how the girls have interpreted his instructions. He ends up by saying that the straw "MUST STAY STACKED." He learned to state his instructions in a positive way instead of a negative way.[4]

Choose Words Carefully, Speak Them Clearly

Sometimes children misunderstand us because they don't know the meaning of the words we use, so they assume we are saying a similar word that they do know.

One little girl heard that a mean teacher at her school had been fired. She went home and told her parents that the supervisor had burned up the mean old teacher.

One family passed a smelly meatpacking plant every Sunday on their way to church. The mother said the bad smell came "from the plant over there." A few years later, on a vacation, they smelled the same bad smell. One of the children pointed to a tall weed and said, "It must come from the plant over there."

Other times, children misunderstand because we don't enunciate our words clearly, or we speak too quickly or softly. A friend of mine grew up in a church where they would often sing the song "Lead On, O King Eternal." He always thought they were saying, "Lead On, O Kinky Turtle."

One five-year-old boy came home from Sunday school asking, "What's a weeklebut?" The child became more and more frustrated when his dad could not tell him. Finally more information came out. "You know," the boy said. "We are weeklebut. He is strong."

This not only happens with young children but with teens and adults as well. I once heard a pastor who said in his sermon, "We all have fallen genes." *Genes* was heard as "jeans," and a muffled laughter spread across the congregation. Then the red-faced pastor laughed as he realized what he had said.

Some misunderstandings are inevitable, but we can minimize them by speaking carefully and clearly.

Use Good Manners

Speak respectfully. Remember "please" and "thank you." Even when you must be firm, be courteous. Never call a child names or belittle him. Our attitude toward children should not be one of condescension, but of respect.

Remember when Jesus' disciples argued over who was the greatest? Jesus took a little child and brought him into their group. Jesus said, "Whoever welcomes this little child in my name welcomes me; and whoever welcomes me welcomes the one who sent me. For he who is least among you all—he is the greatest" (Luke 9:48).

Pay attention to the way you welcome children into your room.

Treat the child as you would treat an adult. Greet him by name. Smile at him. Listen to him. Talk to little ones in a normal tone of voice and not with "baby talk."

Be careful about teasing children. Teasing can make a child confused about what you really mean, and sometimes it is received as mockery and criticism. It can easily make a child feel stupid. We want children to feel loved and valued.

Taking the time and effort to communicate effectively with children will reap great rewards for teachers. After all, we are to reflect Jesus to those around us, including children. Henrietta Meers said, "First I learned to love my teacher. Then I learned to love my teacher's God."[5] That is the goal.

Wired for Learning

Individual Learning Differences

"Where did the thunder go? In back of the world?"
—Four year old

If the stages of a child's development are the framework for this house of faith that we're building, then *learning strengths* are the wiring. *Learning strengths* are factors that motivate a person to learn.

Just as each person has favorite foods, each person also has his favorite ways to learn, although he might not be conscious of it. These are learning strengths. They make it easy for him to learn. They enable, energize, or even motivate him. He is comfortable on these paths of learning. Other paths, which may be preferred by another person, are full of roadblocks for him. God has wired each person differently.

Many researchers have studied the factors that affect the way we learn. The following information is a simplified overview of some of those models.

Sensory Strengths

Dr. Rita Dunn and Dr. Kenneth Dunn are educators who have done extensive research on learning styles. They found that people perceive information *best* when it comes to them through the sense they prefer: auditory, visual, or tactile-kinesthetic.[1]

All preschoolers are tactile-kinesthetic; they learn best when they are touching and moving. But many older children learn best this way too. Among all people over ten years old, forty percent learn best by moving and doing.

Some children in the early elementary stage start showing a preference for visual learning; they learn best by seeing. Among all people over ten years old, forty percent learn best by seeing.

In the older elementary stage, around ten to twelve years old, some children start showing a preference for auditory learning; they learn best by hearing. Among all people over ten years old, twenty percent learn best by hearing.[2]

What does this have to do with our teaching? We tend to teach the way we learn best. That means that if we learn best by hearing, we tend to do most of our teaching by talking. We expect the children to learn by just listening. If we learn best by seeing, we tend to use a lot of visuals. If we learn best by touching and doing, we tend to use lots of active learning.

What about you? Do you like to see charts, diagrams, and maps? Do you like to watch a skill demonstrated before you try it? If your answer is yes, you are probably a visual learner and teacher.

Do you learn best by listening to teachers? Does it help you learn to hear yourself repeat the information? Do you like to learn by discussing issues with others? If your answer is yes, you are probably an auditory learner and teacher.

Do you learn best by trying things yourself? Do you like hands-on learning? Are you good at activities that require movement? If your answer is yes, you are probably a tactile-kinesthetic learner and teacher.

Now you know how you learn best. Think about how you *teach*. Ask yourself if you need to move out of your comfort zone when you teach so you can communicate better to those children who learn differently than you do.

Physical and Environmental Strengths

Dunn and Dunn have found other elements that affect learning. Here are a few.

Physical position affects how well people learn. Some people learn best when they are lying flat on their stomachs. Some learn best when they are sprawled on a soft couch. Some concentrate best when they are sitting straight up.

Movement affects how well people learn. Some people learn best when they are moving. In a traditional classroom setting, these people are constantly swinging a leg back and forth or wiggling a foot or drumming their fingers.

I am a wiggler. When I have to concentrate, it helps if I pace the floor. When I ride my exercise bike, I have to keep a pad of paper and pencil handy because I get all kinds of ideas. Somehow, when my body is moving, my mind is freed to think.

Eating or chewing something helps some people concentrate. What do these kids chew on in traditional classroom settings where they can't have gum or snacks? They chew on their pencils and erasers, or even on scraps of paper! It helps them think!

Sound helps some people. *Silence* helps others. My sister used to come home from school and go into her room to do her homework. Then she'd turn on loud rock music. I never believed that she was studying, because I preferred a quiet environment. But now I know my sister *was* studying! She just did it differently than I did!

Light is a factor in how easily a person learns. Some people learn best when the lights are bright. Some learn best when the lights are dim. Most people learn best in natural daylight. My son's fourth grade teacher knew this, so she talked her school into buying color-corrected, full-spectrum lightbulbs for her classroom. It gave the room the look of being lit by natural daylight. She said she could tell the difference in her students. They were more alert and learned more easily.

Temperature affects how easily a person learns. Some

people learn best when the temperature is cooler and some learn best when it's warmer.

The time of day affects our learning abilities. Some people are morning people; others are night people. Most elementary children learn best between 10 A.M. and 2 P.M.[3]

Design of the room affects how easily people learn. Some people learn best when they're in a formal setting with desks and chairs, but many learn best when they're in an informal setting. It's easier for a person who prefers the formal setting to adapt to the informal setting than the other way around.[4]

Strengths in Style

Bernice McCarthy has studied learning and has found that there are four styles of learning.[5]

The *imaginative* learner approaches what he has to learn by asking the question, "Why?" He wants to know why the lesson is important to him. He learns best when he sees that it has meaning for his life. He likes to work with people.

The *analytic* learner asks, "What?" He wants to know the facts. He likes things organized. He likes to solve problems and find answers. He's a thinker.

The *common-sense* learner asks, "How?" He likes to test the theories and try the ideas. He likes hands-on projects.

The *dynamic* learner asks, "What can become of this?" He likes to brainstorm and try new things. He is creative.

Strengths in Intelligence

The book *Seven Kinds of Smart* by Thomas Armstrong explains researcher Howard Gardner's theory of multiple intelligences. Gardner found that everyone has seven areas of intelligence. People usually operate well in two or three of the seven areas, although they can grow in the other areas as well.[6]

Linguistic. People who are intelligent in the area of linguistics enjoy playing with sounds and words. They learn best by saying, hearing, and seeing words. They enjoy writing, reading, and listening.

Logical-mathematical. People who operate well in the logical-mathematical area of intelligence enjoy exploring patterns and experimenting. They like to reason out problems. They enjoy science kits, brainteasers, computers, and things they can collect and categorize.

Spatial. Spatial people think in pictures. They are basically visual learners. They enjoy films, videos, maps, cameras, building supplies, and art supplies.

Musical. Musical people like humming, singing, and playing instruments. They like listening to music and are sensitive to other sounds around them. They like rhythm and melody. They often learn well when music is playing in the background. They memorize well when they can sing what they're trying to learn.

Bodily-kinesthetic. People who operate well in the bodily-kinesthetic area of intelligence like to learn through their senses. They enjoy anything physical. They touch and move. They like role playing, creative movement, and hands-on activities.

Interpersonal. These people like to organize and communicate. They enjoy other people and have lots of friends. They learn by interacting with others.

Intrapersonal. Intrapersonal people like to work alone. They are self-motivated. They have deep thoughts, ideas, and dreams.[7]

Making It Practical

Now how does all this apply to the classroom? How in the world can we make our classrooms appeal to all these different learners?

The point is to realize how unique each child is. God has

made us all different. So what we have to provide in our classrooms is *variety* and *flexibility*. We provide some activities to see, some to hear, and some to touch and do. We use music and puzzles, videos and role playing. We try to be sensitive to children who like to work in groups and sensitive to children who enjoy working alone. Children are usually willing and able to do activities that don't match a learning preference of theirs if they know that sooner or later they'll get to do something that appeals to them.

Here's how this information became practical to me. When my class has group time, we sit on a rug. There are always a few children who prefer to lie on their stomachs. I let them, as long as they are not disturbing anyone else.

Sometimes I turn the room lights off when telling the Bible story, and use flashlights. We usually have a cooking activity and talk about the story or theme while the children are eating. We sometimes have a tape softly playing background music. We have active times and quiet times. The point is that we have flexibility and variety.

One mother told me how the multiple-intelligence theory affected her sons. Her older son was very strong in the linguistic and logical-mathematical area. He made very good grades in school. Her younger son was not strong in those areas and did not make good grades in school. But he was very strong in the tactile-kinesthetic area. He could catch and throw any kind of ball.

Fortunately, this mother had learned about the theory of multiple intelligence. She told her sons that they were both smart. She emphasized that just because her younger son did not excel in the linguistic and logical-mathematical areas, that did not mean he was not intelligent. He was just intelligent in another area.

So every child is smart. Every child can learn. It is we who must communicate in ways that they can understand.

Chapter 11

Making the Connection

Lively Lessons

A teacher of two year olds was teaching them how to pray.

She would say a phrase, and they would echo her.

At the end of the prayer, she said, "Aw-men."

All the children said, "Aw-men."

Then one little girl said, "And no women."

Learning occurs when experience touches truth. Here's a very simple example. Mommy says, "Keep your hand away from the oven door. The oven gets hot." That is a truth. What happens when the child touches the oven door? He has an experience. He learns a truth: The oven gets hot.

There are some truths we don't want children to experience. We want them to believe us when we tell them it's dangerous to cross a busy street by themselves. We tell them to trust us when we say that drugs will damage their bodies and minds. We don't want them to experience truths in areas that would be destructive to them, so we rely on the relationship of trust that we've built with them. We hope they will trust what we say.

But what about other kinds of life lessons? What about spiritual concepts we want children to learn? We could rely exclusively on verbal communication, but children will learn best if their experience touches the truth we are teaching.

What is an experience? Experience is something that happens to us, and it involves our senses: sight, hearing, smell, taste, and touch. The more of the five senses that are involved, the stronger the experience and the memory of it will be.

The Master Teacher

How do we teach using experience? One way to learn how to do something is to watch an expert do it first. We want to learn how to teach, how to communicate effectively. So let's look at the expert: Jesus, the Master Teacher.

"Jesus was walking by Lake Galilee. He saw two brothers, Simon (called Peter) and Simon's brother Andrew. The brothers were fishermen, and they were fishing in the lake with a net. Jesus said, 'Come follow me. I will make you fishermen for men'" (Matthew 4:18, 19, ICB).

What did Jesus do? He used a sensory experience to teach a truth. What kind of experience did Peter and Andrew have? They could see the sparkling waves of water and the wiggling fish. They could hear the waves sloshing and smacking the sides of the boat. They could feel the rough nets and the wet fish they tossed into the boat. And they could smell the fish. All of this was part of their experience that day.

Then Jesus wove a truth into their experience. He said, "From now on you can fish for men." Why didn't he say, "Follow me, and I will show you how to win souls for God's kingdom"? He was linking the truth to their experience.

Do you suppose that on other occasions when Peter and Andrew saw those same sights and smelled those same smells, their minds went back to the memory of what Jesus had said? Their experience had touched the truth that Jesus was teaching them. They learned that their purpose was to draw people into God's kingdom.

On another occasion, Jesus taught his followers on a hill-side. "Look at the birds in the air," he said. "They don't plant or harvest or store food in barns. But your heavenly Father feeds the birds. And you know that you are worth much more than the birds. You cannot add any time to your life by worrying about it.

"And why do you worry about clothes? Look at the flowers in the field. See how they grow. They don't work or make clothes for themselves. But I tell you that even Solomon with his riches was not dressed as beautifully as one of these flowers. . . . So you can be even more sure that God will clothe you" (Matthew 6:28-30, ICB).

Jesus taught the truth of God's care while his followers experienced nature. They could see and hear the birds. They could smell and touch the flowers. Their experience touched the truth Jesus was teaching them. They learned about God's care.

Matthew 18:2-4 shows Jesus setting up an experience for his followers. "Jesus called a little child to him. He stood the child before the followers. Then he said, 'I tell you the truth. You must change and become like little children. If you don't do this, you will never enter the kingdom of heaven. The greatest person in the kingdom of heaven is the one who makes himself humble like this child'" (ICB).

This child was someone Jesus' followers could see, hear, and touch. Their experience touched the truth Jesus was teaching them. They learned about getting into God's kingdom.

One day, Jesus was traveling through Samaria. He was tired, so he sat down beside a well. It wasn't long until a Samaritan woman came to the well to get water. Jesus asked her for a drink.

The woman was surprised. "How can you ask me for a drink?" she said.

Jesus answered her this way: "You don't know who asked you for a drink. If you knew, you would have asked me, and I would have given you living water" (John 4:10, ICB).

Why didn't Jesus say, "I am the bread of life"? Because she wasn't having an experience with bread. She was having an experience with water. She could smell the dank, wet well. She could hear the splash of her jar dropping into the water. She could hear the water dripping as she pulled the jar up. She could feel the water on her hands. She could see it slosh from side to side in the jar. And she probably tasted some of it to quench her thirst.

Jesus used the woman's experience to teach his truth. Her experience touched his truth, and she learned. How many times after that would she go to the well, draw water, and think about the "living water"?

Perhaps my favorite example of all is in John 13. "It was almost time for the Jewish Passover Feast. . . . During the meal Jesus stood up and took off his outer clothing. Taking a towel, he wrapped it around his waist. Then he poured water into a bowl and began to wash the followers' feet. He dried them with the towel that was wrapped around him" (vv. 1-5, ICB).

Jesus had set up the experience for his disciples this time. They saw him kneel with the towel around his waist and the bowl of water. They felt the cool, wet, cleansing water. They felt the towel massage their tired feet. They heard the water drip back into the bowl. With this experience, Jesus taught them about servanthood. "I did this as an example for you. So you should do as I have done for you" (13:15, ICB).

There is a Chinese proverb that says, "What I hear, I forget. What I see, I remember. What I do, I know." Jesus said, "So you should do as I have done for you." A few verses later, he says, "If you know these things, you will be happy if you do them." Jesus' disciples had experienced with their senses. They heard Jesus' truth. Now they needed to *do*. That is learning.

The Master Teacher

How It's Done

Linking truth to a child's experience is easiest to do if you are the parent. That's because the experiences come naturally. You can do what God told his people to do long ago. "These commandments that I give you today are to be upon your hearts. Impress them on your children. Talk about them when you sit at home and when you walk along the road, when you lie down and when you get up" (Deuteronomy 6:6, 7). You can take the experiences that happen every day and link God's truths to them.

However, in the classroom, we usually have to do it a little bit differently. We set up experiences called *activities* that we will link to the truth we want to teach. We provide activities for the children into which we weave the truth.

One very important area of active learning is in works of service. Children can serve in a variety of real, meaningful ways. They can collect food and make food baskets to take to needy families. They can visit the elderly at home, talk with them, and sing to them. They can help rake leaves and mow lawns. Older children can help teach younger children's classes. There are dozens of ways children can serve! They are learning at the same time and gaining a sense of belonging and competence.

How do we know children are going to learn what we want them to learn from activities? We plan each activity with a purpose in mind. We know how the activity relates to the point we want to get across, the truth we are trying to teach. Knowing this, we ask the children leading questions. We guide their thoughts and conversation during or immediately after the activity. In a lesson plan, this may be called "Discussion" or "Guided Conversation" or "Talk About." That's how we make the connection.

Your Map

How did you come to be a teacher? Here's what traditionally happens to most people. The call goes out at church: There's a need for teachers. You volunteer. Then in a group meeting, or maybe just a spontaneous "meet-you-in-the-hall" meeting with the supervisor, you are handed a booklet and/or a large envelope or box. This is your lesson plan book, a packet of "visuals," and maybe a booklet of "handwork." Your material might include a box of toys instead of the visuals and handwork.

Where do you go from here? First of all, let's take a look at your lesson plan book. It is a part of the curriculum your church has ordered.

Curriculum? What is curriculum? It is a map. It tells you how to get where you want to go. It will have overall goals for your age group, and through the year the lessons will take you to that goal. Lessons are the points of interest you pass as you travel the route on the curriculum map. Each one you pass puts you one step nearer your overall goal. In fact, each of these interest points (or lessons) has goals of its own that fit into the bigger picture.

Lesson plans are simply suggestions for what to do during class time. Not having a lesson plan will make you frustrated. You will have a hard time reaching your goal without a plan. However, being glued or locked into your lesson plan will make you just as frustrated, because the people who write lesson plans cannot know your specific situation.

Your situation is different from my situation. Even your own situation may change from year to year. I have used the same curriculum, the same lesson plans, for eight years now. Each year has been different.

One year I had twelve children in my class. The next year I had twenty-eight. One year I had a class with children from several different countries. Another year I had a child who used a wheelchair. One year the kids listened eagerly at group time. The next year, they were into rough-and-tumble wrestling instead of listening.

I've taught in tiny classrooms and huge classrooms. I've taught in churches with few materials available to me, and I've taught in other churches with resource centers where the workers had my requested materials stacked and ready to go when I dropped by before class. I've taught in situations where I had only forty-five minutes to complete the activities. I've taught in classes where I had ninety minutes of class time.

Can one lesson plan cover all these possibilities? No. That's why a lesson plan is a group of suggestions for you. When you get your lesson plan, read it and ask yourself some questions:

- Does this fit my class's needs?

- Does this fit the time schedule I have?
- Does this fit the materials available to me?
- Does this fit the abilities and interests of my kids?
- Does this fit the space available to me?

Then delete and add activities according to your answers to these questions.

How do I find activities to add? You need resource books. Good activity books broaden your choices. You may also think of some activities on your own. If you are really going to be child sensitive, you'll opt for more original arts and crafts and fewer lick-and-stick activities. (Lick-and-stick activities require no original thinking, and everyone's picture looks just alike.)

You will also use those visuals sparingly because there are many more active, interesting and fun ways to involve the children in the lesson. The last thing you want to do is bore the children. God is not boring. Life in him is an adventure, so learning about him should be an adventure too.

If you're excited about what's going on in class, chances are the children will be excited too. If you're bored with it, chances are *they'll* be bored. Ask, "How can I use my special gifts and talents to enhance this lesson? How can I make it exciting?"

For example, if you're a good cook, you could do a cooking activity with the children. If you're a gardener, you might bring some flowers to examine or some seedlings to plant. What do you have that would help communicate the theme of the lesson?

As you think about the activities you need, just remember to "Take AIM." Make your lessons

Active,
Interesting,
Meaningful.

Kids want to be where the action is. Where the excitement is. Where it matters. Where you care. And they know you care when you spend the time to help them enjoy the lesson through active, interesting, meaningful activities.

The Five-Day Sandwich

Telling Bible Stories Creatively

A young boy listened as his teacher told the story of the good Samaritan. When a character passed by the hurt man, she made the hurt man call, "Help!" But with each person that passed, the "Help!" got softer and weaker until the man's cries could hardly be heard. After church, the boy's mother asked him what he had learned in class. The boy said, "I learned that you gotta call for help louder than that!"

There was once a wealthy traveler who went on an African adventure tour. One day, his tour took him to a remote tribal village where there was no electricity. The wealthy traveler felt sorry for the people who lived in the village, so he paid to have electricity brought to the village and shipped a television set to every hut.

A few years later, the wealthy traveler had an opportunity to visit this same village again. To his surprise, he found all the television sets piled into one large hut.

He asked the head man, "Why do you not use your televisions?"

The head man answered, "Because we have a storyteller."

"But TV knows thousands of stories," said the traveler.

"That's true," said the head man. "But the storyteller knows us."

George Gerbner, a researcher of the role of media in our culture, says, "Whoever tells the stories controls how children grow up. . . . Television now tells most of the stories."[1]

It's true that television tells most of the stories. But there is still a tremendous attraction to the storyteller in person, as the legend of the African tribe illustrates. Jim Trelease, author of *The Read-Aloud Handbook,* writes, "If a plastic box in your living room can turn on your child to chocolate breakfast cereal, then you should be able to do ten times as much—because you are a sensitive, loving, and caring human being."[2]

Stories are powerful. Storytelling is powerful. Yet the Bible story is often the most overlooked and ho-hum part of the Sunday school hour.

One well-worn technique of storytelling in Sunday school is for the teacher to read the story aloud from the teacher's guide, which is on her lap in front of her. Meanwhile, she moves figures on a flannel board according to the directions she's reading. It's no wonder children get restless and bored. If you use this technique, realize that this is a starting point. Let's grow and move on from there.

Dr. Howard Hendricks, author of *The Seven Laws of the Teacher*, writes, "We teach Bible stories as if the people were cardboard characters who had none of the feelings, thoughts and problems we do."[3]

Robert Coles, author of *The Spiritual Life of Children*, was asked why he says biblical stories aren't always interesting to young people today. His answer was, "Because they're not presented as stories by and about human beings. They're abstracted and presented in an unreal world in which religion equals some kind of Sunday-at-11 duty and obligation. . . . If the story is told with conviction and aimed at their hearts, they'll listen."[4]

Our Heritage of Story

What is storytelling? Let's first define it by what it is not. Storytelling is not reading. Storytelling is breathing life into characters. "And the Lord God formed man from the dust of the ground and breathed into his nostrils the breath of life, and man became a living being" (Genesis 2:7). What God did literally, the storyteller does figuratively. We make these people come alive in the child's mind, in his imagination.

Why? Peninnah Schram, a Jewish storyteller, puts it this way: "When a generation can feel its ancestors' feelings, share their ideas and sorrows, the lessons of their lives will live on."[5] Many cultures, including the Jewish culture, have preserved a body of stories, handed down from generation to generation. These stories serve to give them a cultural sense of heritage. These are their roots.

All of us who have been born again into God's kingdom now have the heritage of his people. Ephesians 1:5 says that God "predestined us to be adopted as his sons through Jesus Christ, in accordance with his pleasure and will." Romans 11 tells us that the Jews were like an olive tree, and we are like wild olive shoots that have been "grafted in among the others" and now share "in the nourishing sap from the olive root" (v. 17).

So we are God's people. And the stories of his people are the stories of our ancestors. As Peninnah Schram says, we must feel our ancestors' feelings, share their ideas and sorrows, so the lessons of their lives can live on.

"O my people," said God. "Hear my teaching; listen to the words of my mouth. I will open my mouth in parables. I will utter things hidden from of old—what we have heard and known, what our fathers have told us. We will not hide them from their children; we will tell the next generation the praiseworthy deeds of the Lord, his power, and the wonders he has done. He decreed statutes for Jacob and established the law in Israel, which he commanded our forefathers to teach their children, so the next generation would know them, even the children yet to be born, and they in turn would tell their children. Then they would put their trust in God and would not forget his deeds, but would keep his commands" (Psalm 78:1-7).

The patriarchs kept their history alive. Their storytelling passed on the heritage of God's people. We forget that in the history of the world, more years have been spent without printing or the widespread ability to read and write than with these blessings. But because the written story is so accessible and commonplace, we often see it as mundane and boring.

Storytelling is a shared experience. The storyteller is a tour guide, taking the listeners on a tour of the story. And in our case, the story is God's story, the truth of how God deals with his people. It's the perfect blending of knowing Bible facts and learning how God works in our daily lives. That's all the more reason to make the story exciting for the listeners.

Amat Victoria Curam

The Latin expression "Amat Victoria Curam" means "Victory loves preparation." If you are going to have a successful time in the classroom, there must be preparation. How do you prepare for communicating the story? When Jack Maguire, a professional storyteller, teaches people to tell stories, he takes them through five steps.[6] I've taken these steps a bit further and have made them into what I call a Five-Day Sandwich.

To build the Five-Day Sandwich, you add one ingredient each day for five days. All you need is five or ten minutes a day to build this sandwich, although you can spend longer if you'd like. Try to work this into your regular schedule, doing it at the same time each day. Any time is fine. My best scheduled time is the ten minutes at night just before going to bed.

Take five days to "build the sandwich" and one day to teach the story. Since there are seven days in a week, that leaves one day of "grace," so that you have room to forget, or to be too busy, or too tired, or whatever else comes up.

Begin learning next week's story on the day after you have taught. For example, if you teach on Sunday, look at next week's lesson plan on Monday. Try to start learning the story for next week. This gives you an entire week to think about what you might do during your next lesson. For example, as you read the next lesson, let's say you think of a wonderful activity you could do. It requires balloons. Now you have time to get balloons at the store. If you had kept the lesson book closed until Saturday night, you wouldn't have had time.

Or you may be in the grocery store, passing the bin of oranges. "Hey!" you think. "I could use a couple of these for next week's lesson." If you don't know what the lesson is for next week, opportunities like this can't happen.

Now let's build that sandwich! Here are the ingredients.

1. Enjoy

The meat of the sandwich is the story itself. So on the first day, read the story for your next lesson from the Bible. Read it simply to *enjoy* it and relate it to your life. Does it have a meaning for you? Does God want to tell you something from this passage?

2. Character

This is the cheese on our sandwich. You will read the passage again the second day. But this time take a good look at each main *character*. Close your eyes. What do you think this character looked like? If you were with him on this occasion, what would his voice sound like? If you shook hands with him, what would his handshake feel like? How would he walk? Does he have a smell about him? Practice this now with the story of David and Goliath. David's handshake would certainly be different from Goliath's!

You won't go into the classroom and tell the children, "David was five feet ten. He had wavy brown hair and dark brown eyes." You won't fictionalize. You will only tell the facts as the Bible tells them. The point is for you to start thinking of the characters as real flesh-and-blood people because they *were*. And if you can start feeling like they are real, you will tell your stories with more excitement. You will be animated about it. You will tell the story as if the characters were real, living, breathing people in a real, hot and cold, up and down, quiet and noisy world.

You can do some of these exercises with the children in class. You can ask them to imagine what David must have been like. Ask them what they think Goliath looked like. It will help *them* to start thinking of these characters as the real people they were.

3. Phrases

Here is the onion to put on the sandwich. You will read the same passage the third day, this time reading for any *phrase* that you might need to memorize. Your aim is not to memorize the story word-for-word, but to retell it in your own words. However, if the story contains the memory verse for the lesson, you should memorize it. You will want to say it word-for-word in the story at the right time.

In some stories, you'll find special phrases that give the story a spark. You should also memorize these. For example, in the story of David and Goliath, I would memorize what David said to Goliath: "You come against me with sword and spear and javelin, but I come against you in the name of the Lord." This is a powerful part of the story.

Another phrase, a very simple one, comes in the story of Gideon. Gideon's small army surrounds the enemy. It's night. Everyone is watching Gideon and waiting . . . waiting . . . waiting. Then Gideon blows his trumpet, breaks his pitcher, and holds out his torch. His soldiers blow their trumpets, break their pitchers, and hold their torches high. Then they shout, "A sword for the Lord and for Gideon!" I yell this phrase right there in the classroom. It makes everyone want to jump up and shout, "Yes! Hooray for Gideon!" It's exciting. And it should be!

You can use your God-given voice to great advantage in storytelling. You can yell as I do in the story of Gideon. (Practice at home when no one's around.) Or you can whisper loudly. I do this when I'm telling something that happens at night. Or maybe it's something suspenseful. Lower your voice. The children will get as quiet as can be just to hear you.

You can also speak slowly. I do this when I tell about Abraham sitting outside his tent on a very hot day; if it's a very hot day, nobody is moving very fast. Or you can speak very quickly. Do this when someone is running or riding along quickly in a chariot. Maybe there's a storm and you want to build tension by speaking urgently and quickly.

You can make the pitch of your voice go up if someone is climbing up a tree or going up a mountain. Or you can start high and make your voice go lower if someone is coming down a mountain. Try some different skills with your voice and incorporate them into your storytelling.

4. Environment

This is the tomato for your sandwich. As you read the same passage on the fourth day, pay attention to the *environment*, the setting of the story. Occasionally the biblical account tells what the weather was like, but often we are not told very much about the environment. The previous example of Abraham showed him sitting outside on a hot day. His tent was near the trees of Mamre. We know there were trees, there was a tent, and it was a hot day.

So again, close your eyes. What do you know about Bible lands? What do you think it was like? Is the landscape rocky, sandy, forested, a meadow? Is there a lake or pond or ocean? Whatever the story, imagine yourself there. What do you see? What do you hear? Birds? Wind? Thunder? A brook? An army? A crowd of people coming down the road? What do you smell? Do you smell the dinner that Martha is cooking? What is the weather and the temperature?

Again, you will not tell children something that is not fact. But you can start making it real to yourself. What must it have been like?

5. Total

Now we put the lettuce on the sandwich. On the fifth day, read through the story passage again. You will probably enjoy it more than you did the first time you read it because now you have made it seem real. And it *was* real once upon a time! It did happen to real people in a real place, just as real as where you are right now. Isn't God wonderful and amazing as he works among his people?

The key to successful storytelling is believability. Make it believable. Be excited to share this story. Remember: If you're not excited, the children won't be excited.

Prayer

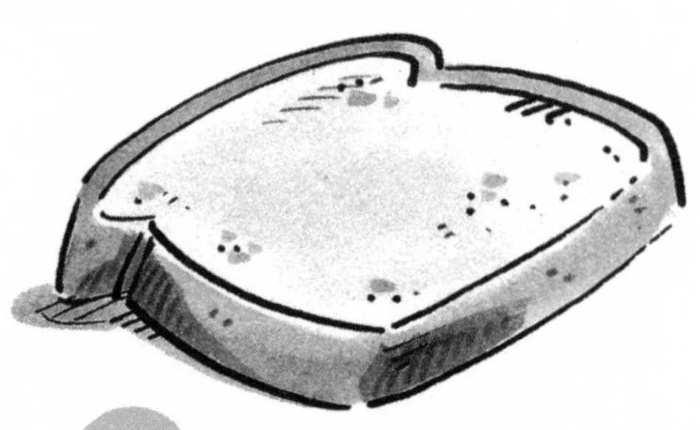

But something is missing from this sandwich. What is it? We have meat, cheese, onion, tomato, and lettuce. We need bread. Sandwich all of the steps in *prayer*. Pray before you begin. Pray after you've finished. And why not go ahead and pile this sandwich high? Pray in between too. Let the Lord guide your preparation and touch your own heart with what he wants you to glean from this passage.

The Five-Day Sandwich

Story Material

Storytelling purists say that the only way to be true to real storytelling tradition is to tell the story without any props, using only your voice and body movements. But that's not what we're interested in for our classes. There are many kinds of materials you can use to help you tell stories. As you plan the story, think of the materials you have access to.

You can use the traditional flannel figures. These are always good for children to use to retell the story themselves later in the class time, but be careful not to use flannel figures all the time. Vary the materials you use from week to week, so the children always wonder what exciting and fun things you have planned for them today. If they seem bored with one method, don't use it. Opt for something else.

Puppets are fun. They can be store-bought or homemade. One easy way to make hand puppets is to staple two paper plates together and draw a face on one side. Then insert your hand between the two plates. Your wrist becomes the neck of the puppet.

You can also use story pictures. The smaller the group, the more intricate and detailed the picture can be. For larger groups, simpler pictures with bold lines and colors are better so everyone can see. But be careful. Just as with flannel figures, it's easy to get in the habit of relying on story pictures. A steady diet of these becomes dull. There are so many other exciting ways to get the children actively into the story that you may never even need flannel figures and story pictures. The key is to choose methods you can get excited about.

You can use blocks or boxes. Let children build the houses or the tower or the city that you will use when telling the story. Try using children's toy figures to represent Bible characters. Tell the story in a box of sand or tell it with figures in a tub of water if the setting is on a lake.

Children usually enjoy acting out the story. Let them dress up in old sheets, towels, and pillowcases with armholes cut in them. For younger children, it helps if the teacher narrates and moves the children around where he wants them to stand. Blue sheets can be large rivers or seas. Pitch a tent in the room when you tell stories of Abraham. Bring stuffed animals to help tell the story of Noah or the story of creation. Baby powder is a fun addition to your storytelling kit. Sprinkle some baby powder on children's arms to represent leprosy. When the "lepers" are made well, let the children rub their arms to rub off the powder.

Stories for Older Children

Let older children draw a mural "backdrop" to set the stage for the story. Let them look up geographical and historical details about the story. Find out what's happening in that part of the world today. For these story-related activities, the teachers may need to be resource people, finding and providing these details at one or more "information stations."

One interesting possibility for story exploration for older students is to set up a "jigsaw" classroom. This term was coined by educator Eliot Aronson for use in his public school classrooms. But the concept can also be used to study the Bible. Children are divided into groups, three or four students to a group. Each group is like a separate jigsaw puzzle. Each member of the group is one of the puzzle pieces.

Each member of the group becomes a reporter and is given a different assignment. For example, the first member of each group is to find out what happened to Paul in Lystra and Derbe. Another member of the group finds out where these cities would be located on a globe today. The third child finds out what kind of transportation they had in those days. A fourth could find out about the climate.

You provide the resources for them to research what they need to know. The resources could be simple information pages that you have posted at different parts of the room.

You give the children time to accomplish their assignments, then they meet back in their original group (the "jigsaw" puzzle comes together) and they teach each other within their group.

Older children could publish a newspaper in which they write about the Bible stories as if they were current events. They could write a commercial for the story. They could act out the story and videotape it. They could narrate the story on audio tape, complete with different voices and sound effects. They could write letters about the story to the story's character. They could write a journal as if they were traveling with the story character—Joseph, for example. They could write or tell a sequel to the story. They can practice telling the story and then go to a younger classroom and tell the story there.

Be creative. The difficulty in telling Bible stories is that many of the children have heard them again and again. Finding new and interesting ways to tell these wonderful stories is a challenge. But Jesus said, "Every teacher . . . who has been instructed about the kingdom of heaven is like the owner of a house who brings out of his storeroom new treasures as well as old" (Matthew 13:52).

Remember, we are not telling the story just for the story's sake alone. We are telling the story to see in it a truth that is relevant to the child's life. Get to the issues that affect the children of that age. Then let the kids discuss these real life issues.

Our Own Stories

There is another kind of storytelling that should go on at home and in the Sunday school classroom: sharing our own stories. When a child tells you about his lost cat, or his new shoes, or his grandma's visit, or his winning ball team, he is telling you a story of his life. You can tell the children some of your stories too.

After he healed a demon-possessed man, Jesus told the man, "Return home and tell how much God has done for you" (Luke 8:39). Tell the children what the Lord did for you this week. Then ask, "What did the Lord do for you today?" God and his kingdom are current as well as historical, so we need to tell the current stories too.

"We will tell the next generation the praiseworthy deeds of the Lord, his power, and the wonders he has done" (Psalm 78:4).

Chapter 13

Keep It in Mind

Scripture Memory

A four year old came out of Sunday school saying his memory verse, "Children, obey your carrots."

In one of my favorite picture books, *Wilfrid Gordon McDonald Partridge* by Mem Fox, Wilfrid Gordon's best friend at the old people's home has lost her memory. Wilfrid is not very old, and he doesn't understand. So he asks all his friends at the old people's home, "What's a memory?" Each person he asks tells him something different.[1]

What *is* a memory?

Scientists would tell us that memory involves chemical and physical changes in nerve cells in the brain. Memory is centered in the cerebral cortex, which controls functions like problem solving and language. By the time a child is three years old, his brain is seventy-five to eighty percent of its adult size. But he's growing quickly. By the time he's four, his brain is ninety percent of its adult size. This means there are more connections between parts of the brain. More connections mean increased alertness, attention, and memory.

Psychologists would tell us that there are basically three kinds of memory. First, there's sensory memory. This comes to you through one or more of your senses. But it's the kind of memory that you hold in your mind for only an instant after you experience it. Then it's gone.

The second kind of memory is short-term memory. This is the kind of memory you hold in your mind as long as you are actively thinking about it. For example, you look up a phone number and repeat it to yourself as you walk to the phone and dial the number. By the time you've finished your conversation and hung up, you've forgotten the number. It lasts in your mind only about twenty seconds.

The third kind of memory is long-term memory. Some of this kind of memory can last the rest of your life. One way something can enter your long-term memory is by intense emotions. I don't remember many things before I turned five. But I vividly remember two events. I remember dropping a milk bottle on my toe. (This was in the "olden" days of glass milk bottles.) And I remember sitting on my porch with my grandmother when there were yellow jackets buzzing around. The first event was planted in my mind because of pain. The second entered because of fear.

Another way something can get into your long-term memory is by repetition. Did you ever move to a new town? When you drove to the church or the ballpark or the mall for the first time, you may have had to follow a map. You had to read street signs and look for landmarks. But you drove there time after time. Then one day, you started out from your house and the next thing you knew, you were at your destination. You had simply driven the correct streets to get there! The repetition of driving that route had stored it in your long-term memory.

Much of the learning we do from birth throughout the rest of our lives comes from repetition. We do something so often that it becomes automatic to us. But there is another kind of repetition that stores memory. That's rote memory.

Rote memory is defined as mindless repetition—something that's repeated mechanically or without understanding. This is the kind of repetition kids do in school to make a good grade on the test, but they forget it as soon as the test is over. We might even call it mid-term memory, because it's longer than short-term memory, but shorter than long-term memory. We hold onto the information as long as it serves a purpose. When it ceases to serve the purpose, we drop it.

Did you memorize the states of the U.S. and their capitals when you were in school? Say them now. Did you memorize the presidents of the United States? List them. Did you memorize the Gettysburg address or the Preamble to the U.S. Constitution? Say them. Do you remember them? Or did you forget? Why?

Try another experiment. How many Scriptures did you memorize as you grew up? How many can you say now? Why do you remember the ones you remember?

Why Teach Memory Verses?

When we see how much of God's Word we memorized and how little we remember, we might ask why we should memorize the Scriptures at all. You might especially ask that question if you had difficulty memorizing, or if you never got the prize, or if the teacher or class put you down when you failed to learn your Scripture for the day. But there are some important reasons to memorize Scripture.

Meditation

David was called "a man after [God's] own heart" (1 Samuel 13:14). How was he able to be so close to God? I think one of the reasons is found in Psalm 145:5. David said, "I will meditate on your wonderful works." In Psalm 143:5, 6 David said, "I remember the days of long ago; I meditate on all your works and consider what your hands have done. I spread out my hands to you; my soul thirsts for you like a parched land." David was serious about seeking God.

Meditating on God's Word means deliberately and consciously considering it. It's turning God's Word over and over in your thoughts, pouring through it, "bathing" in it. It's much easier to do that when it's in your heart or you are in the process of putting it in your heart. Psalm 119 is full of verses about meditating on God's precepts, decrees, and promises.

Fighting Temptation

Another reason to memorize Scripture is to fight temptation. Psalm 119:11 says, "I have hidden your word in my heart that I might not sin against you." Ephesians 6:17 tells us that God's Word is the sword of the Spirit. Luke 4 shows us how Jesus used this sword to fight temptation. When the devil tempted Jesus, he fought back by quoting Scripture. If Jesus did it, we should too. And we need to equip children to fight temptation in this way.

Prayer

A third reason to memorize Scripture is to use it in prayer. First John 5:14, 15 says, "This is the confidence we have in approaching God: that if we ask anything according to his will, he hears us. And if we know that he hears us—whatever we ask—we know that we have what we asked of him." How do we know we are asking according to his will? One of the surest ways is to pray Scripture. "Lord, you are my shepherd. I shall lack nothing. Make me lie down in green pastures. Lead me beside quiet waters. Restore my soul." (See Psalm 23).

Guidance

Another reason to memorize Scripture is to be able to rely on it during life's experiences. There was a very quiet, shy little boy in one of my four-year-old classes. We had been memorizing the verse "I know that God can do all things" (Job 42:2). One evening his mother peeked into the classroom before class time. She said, "Today Timothy came up to me, pointed to the sky, and said, 'Mommy, I know that God up there can do all things.'" The verse had jumped out of the classroom and had found its way into his everyday life.

Another little girl in my class was playing at home with

her two-year-old sister. They were in the yard, and a bee flew near. Her little sister ran into the house crying, afraid of the bee. The big sister ran in after her, calling, "Remember: In God I trust; I will not be afraid" (Psalm 56:11). She was applying her memory verse to a life experience.

One pastor tells the story of his grown daughter who had run away from home and gotten into drugs and prostitution. At the lowest point in her life, she found herself in a run-down trailer, hungry and friendless. She lay in bed all day, and the thing that kept running through her mind was a memory verse she had learned in Sunday school when she was four years old. God used that verse to point her toward home. She went back home and started a new life in the Lord.

So the question is not if we *should* memorize Scripture. The question is *how* we should memorize Scripture so that we can really remember it.

Keys to Memorization

As teachers, we usually expect children to memorize without teaching them how. We just say, "Here's your memory verse for next week. Be sure to learn it so you can say it and get your prize." But if we really think that memorizing Scripture is important, we will do some things in class to help kids learn the Scripture.

Focus on it.

The first thing anyone must do to memorize something is to focus on it. Think about it. It's important to spend some of your class time focusing on the verse.

Link it to something they already know.

Ask yourself how this verse relates to the children. What do they know that you can link it to? For example, "I know that God can do all things." How does that relate to a four year old? The key is in the word "do." What is a four year old able to do?

What is he not able to do? A four year old's world consists of what he can and can't do. God is able to *do* anything.

Help them understand what they are memorizing.

Frank Smith, in his book *Insult to Intelligence*, says, "Rote memorization is the worst strategy for trying to learn anything we do not understand. . . . Learning by rote is the hardest and most pointless way to learn. Students who use memorized formulas without understanding commit monumental mistakes without suspecting their errors."[2] If children are going to memorize, they must understand what they're memorizing.

I was leading a seminar in Houston during which I was actually teaching a group of five year olds while the parents and teachers looked on. Later, we talked about what I did and why I did it, and even analyzed the mistakes I made. During the session with the children, I was teaching the verse, "Be quick to listen and slow to speak" (James 1:19). While I was talking to the children, I realized that though this was a very simple verse, they were not understanding. So I asked them what it meant. They said it meant, "T-a-l-k r-e-a-l s-l-o-w." Needless to say, I had some explaining to do.

Remember the ages at which children come to understand symbolism. Before presenting a memory verse to children, ask yourself if you think they will understand it. Many Bible verses contain symbolic language. Children will find it easier to memorize these verses if you discuss them first and clear up any misunderstandings.

Make it relevant to the child.

We remember the concepts and facts that we use often. They are relevant to us. I remember lots of grammar rules because I use them every day when I write and speak. But I don't remember the theories about geometry. I never need them, so I never use them. Make sure the verses you teach relate to the child's life.

For the young child, my philosophy is "Remember a few rather than forget many." I choose only four to six verses for young children to learn for the entire year. I'd rather they leave my class really knowing four verses than learn a verse each week, none of which they remember after they move on. As they grow older, they can be expected to learn more verses.

In first through third grade, children should still have more oral memory work than written memory work, because many of them are still struggling with reading and writing.

What are some practical ways we can help children learn memory verses? Remember the three sensory areas in which people learn: auditory, visual, and tactile-kinesthetic. Try teaching the verse in an auditory way to help the auditory learner memorize it. Try teaching it in a visual way to help the visual learner. Try teaching it in a tactile-kinesthetic way to help the tactile-kinesthetic learner.

Ideas for the Ears

Children who learn best by listening will be able to memorize by repeating the verse over and over again. They can learn from hearing themselves or someone else say it. It will help if each time you say the verse, you use the same inflection and rhythm. For example, "I know . . . that God . . . can do ALL things."

Sometimes it's fun to repeat the verse in different voices. Say it in a low voice. Say it in a high voice. Say it softly. Shout it. Say it in different accents. Say it like you think a cat would talk. Or try getting faster and faster each time you repeat the verse, until you can't say it intelligibly anymore.

If any of the children have watches that can be set to beep every hour on the hour, you might suggest that they set their watches for that function. Then every time their watch beeps, they say the verse.

Singing the memory verse may help auditory learners.

Perhaps you can make up a tune or put the words to a tune you already know. Or let the children put the verse to music.

Ideas for the Eyes

Visual learners will memorize more easily if they can see something that will help them learn. They might actually visualize the words in the written verse. Or they might organize a verse that is a list by putting the first letter of each word together to see what it spells. I learned Philippians 4:8 this way. I learned the words TNR PLA EP (tenor play E.P.) "Finally, brothers, whatever is **T**rue, whatever is **N**oble, whatever is **R**ight, whatever is **P**ure, whatever is **L**ovely, whatever is **A**dmirable—if anything is **E**xcellent or **P**raiseworthy—think about such things."

Or try a simple game. Get some index cards and write one word of the verse on each card. Then lay the cards out in order so that the children can read the verse. Read through it together. Then ask one child to pick any card and turn it over. Read it together again, supplying the missing word when you come to it. Ask another child to turn over any card. Read it again, this time saying both missing words. Keep going this way until all the cards are turned over and you are all still "reading" the verse.

This same game can be done on the chalkboard or dry erase board, erasing one word at a time. Or, instead of writing the words on cards, write them with a permanent marker on inflated balloons. To "erase" a word, the child must pop the balloon. You can furnish a pin for this, or you can tell the children to sit on the balloons to pop them.

Ideas for the Hands

Sometimes you can put hand motions to the verse. Our class did this with the verse "Love the Lord with all your heart and soul and strength" (Deuteronomy 6:5). When we said *love,* we put our hands on our hearts. When we said *Lord,* we pointed up. When we said *heart* and *soul,* our hands went back over our hearts. When we said *strength,* we made muscles with our upper arms like strong men.

Another fun way to be tactile-kinesthetic with memory work is to toss a beach ball. Whomever the ball is thrown to says the first word of the verse. He then throws it to another person who says the next word and so on until the entire verse has been said. A variation of this is for the child who catches the ball to say the whole verse, then throw it to another child who says the whole verse, and so on.

You could write each word of the verse on an index card, then mix up the cards and ask the children to arrange them in order. A more active, fun way is to pin the cards on the backs of children and then ask one or two other children to arrange the "pinned" children in order. Or hang the scrambled cards on a clothesline that's been strung across the room. Or write the words on paper cups and form teams, seeing which team can arrange their cups in the proper verse order first.

Then there are traditional games you can play using words of the verse. Make a hopscotch path with one word written in each square. Then play hopscotch. Or play "London Bridge." The person who gets "caught" must say the verse. Or play "Duck, Duck, Goose," but with each tap of the head, a word of the verse is said. On the last word of the verse, the one tapped chases the tapper to see who can get back to the spot first.

God's Reminders

As you can see, many of these ideas are combinations of things that appeal to auditory, visual, and tactile-kinesthetic learners. The variations of what you can do are endless.

God uses all of these ways to help his people remember

things. He uses auditory methods. Exodus 17 tells about the time Joshua led God's people out to fight. Moses was watching from a mountain. When Moses held his hands up, God's people would win. Aaron and Hur ended up supporting Moses' hands when Moses got tired. Joshua and his army won. "Then the Lord said to Moses, 'Write this on a scroll as something to be remembered and make sure that Joshua *hears* it'" (Exodus 17:14). And at one time, God told Moses to write down a song so the events would not be forgotten (Deuteronomy 31:19-22).

God also uses visual methods. He set the rainbow in the sky to remind him never again to destroy the earth with water (Genesis 9:12-17). When the Israelites crossed the Jordan River, God told the people to take stones from the river bed and put them at their camp. God said, "These stones are to be a memorial to the people of Israel forever." He said that when the children asked about them, the people were to tell about crossing the Jordan (Joshua 4).

God uses tactile-kinesthetic methods. During the Feast of Booths, the people were to make and live in booths for seven days to help them remember how they had wandered in the wilderness for forty years. For us, the wine and bread of the Communion, or Lord's Supper, and the water of baptism are tactile reminders of what Jesus did for us.

Chapter 14

An Ounce of Prevention

Discipline—Directing the Child

"Don't be a bully and boss around
Like kids that you have found.
Be nice and good and you will find
There'll be less troubles in your mind."
—Eight year old

Discipline is *discipling,* making disciples or followers. I like the word *discipling* because it puts the focus on the teacher or parent. The goal of discipling someone is to help them grow to be like their teacher. This is a big responsibility. It starts with us. Do we want them to be like us? Are we growing to be more like Jesus every day? We must be disciplined first. Children will copy what we do and echo what we say.

Discipline is guiding children to follow a controlled path. At first, the controls are external. Parents and teachers make the rules for the child. But the goal is to bring the child to the place where he is self-controlled. This is a process, as we saw when we looked at the moral development of the child in the first few chapters of this book.

Discipling requires an investment from the adult.

Discipling takes

- prayer
- time
- effort and energy
- wisdom and thought
- sacrifice
- goals
- understanding
- respect
- relationship

There are two other necessary ingredients for discipling:

- consistency
- love

Discipline is a two-sided coin. One side is direction and the other is correction. A ship captain directs his ship toward its destination. We direct a child toward his destination: self-control. But if the ship gets off course, if it goes the wrong direction, the captain must make a course correction to get it back on the right course. So a child must correct his course if he has gone the wrong direction. Children often need help with this. That's where we come in.

Guidance

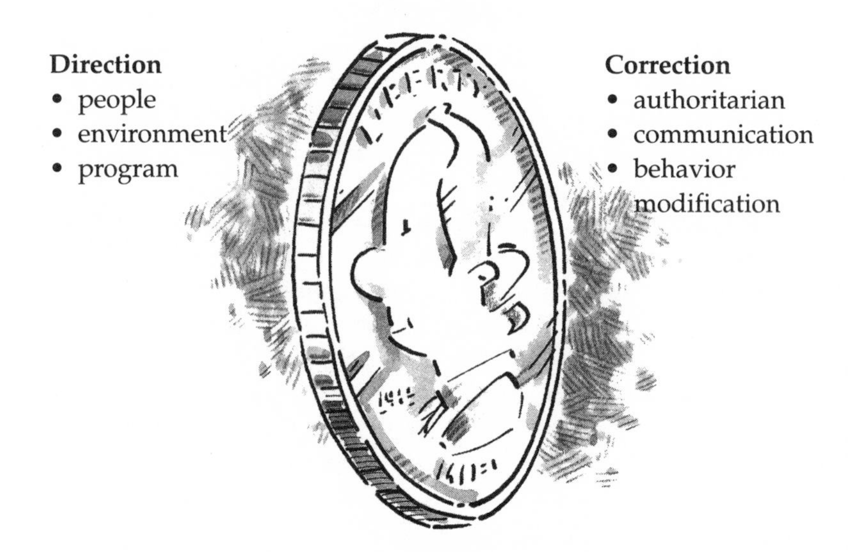

Direction

Believe it or not, all that you have read in this book so far has to do with discipline. That's because it all has to do with setting a positive direction for your class. Positive direction helps prevent the need for correction.

Let's review some of the factors that keep us headed in the right direction:

• Stop, look, and listen. Observe the children in your class. Listen to them.

• Build a relationship with the children. A good relationship helps build trust. And according to pediatrician William Sears, "Respect for authority is based on trust."[1]

• Know what age-appropriate behavior to expect from your children. Review the chapters on development as often as you need to.

• Communicate in ways that your children will understand.

• Have a plan, and then take AIM. Make your lessons **A**ctive, **I**nteresting, and **M**eaningful.

• Make variety the key when choosing activities.

• Make variety and believability the key when telling Bible stories.

• Be excited about your class. If you're not excited, then change what you can to get excited about it.

Let's look at some other specifics in the area of direction and prevention. Grace Mitchell, in her book *A Very Practical Guide to Discipline With Young Children,* suggests that we anticipate behavior problems by looking at possible triggers in three areas: people, environment, and program.[2] Do a checkup by asking yourself some questions about each of these areas.

People: Teacher, Children, and Parents

Do you, as the teacher, arrive early for class? When the teacher is there before the children arrive, the teacher sets the tone for what will happen in the classroom. The children enter the teacher's territory, and the teacher is in charge. But if the children arrive before the teacher does, the children set the tone for what will happen. The teacher enters the children's territory. Who's in charge then?

Are you prepared? It's hard for you to greet children when you're running around looking for the red construction paper and scissors, or punching out the handwork for the day. Some children misbehave to get attention, and the busy-with-materials-teacher is creating a situation that invites this child to misbehave.

Do you pray for the children during the week? Take a list of the children's names home with you, and post it where it will remind you to pray for them and their families. While you are greeting children and visiting with them before class, place a hand on each child and say a silent, short prayer for him. No one even needs to be aware of what you're doing. You can also do this during class activities.

Do you love the children? Dr. Slonecker, a respected pediatrician says, "Tell the child every class time, 'I love you.' If he understands you love him, you'll be able to discipline him better."[3] That's because when children feel loved by someone, they want to please that person. "Every child really wants . . . approval of a favorite adult," writes Grace Mitchell.[4]

Do certain children always misbehave when they're around each other? If you can, separate the children who tempt each other to misbehave. Sometimes this means placing two friends at opposite sides of the story rug, because they are so friendly that they whisper and giggle when it's time to listen. Or it may involve two rough-and-tumble little boys (or girls) who itch to wrestle every time they're near each other. It's not that these children are intentionally trying to disrupt the class.

They are following their natural instincts to have a good time with good friends. Anticipate this temptation and separate the children into different groups or areas if you can.

Do you tell children when they have choices and when they don't? If you don't want the child to choose, don't give him a choice. For example, let's say you want the children to put the blocks away and gather on the rug for story time. Avoid asking, "Would you like to come hear a story now?" because someone will answer "No." You have given him a choice. Instead, say, "It's time to put the blocks away and come to the rug for a story."

Do you give advance warning when activities are going to change? It's always good to let kids know before you change. For example, say, "In five minutes, we'll put the blocks away and come to the story rug." You don't like someone to come up to you when you are busy and say, "Come on, let's go! Right now!" If you can give advance notice, then do. It's part of being respectful.

Are you specific? If we say, "Put that over there," the child may put something else somewhere else because we weren't specific. Later, we see "that" was not put over "there," and we think the child has not obeyed. If only we had been specific, the child would have known that we meant for him to put the toy truck on the bottom shelf.

Have you communicated the rules to the children? We can't expect children to keep the rules if they don't know what the rules are.

Are parents treated with respect? Are they kept informed about what is going on in the classroom? Are they consulted when you have a problem or question about a child?

Environment

Is your room too open? I used to teach in a small classroom. I would look longingly down the hall at a nice big classroom that the kindergartners used. I would think, *Wouldn't it be nice to have a spacious classroom like that?* The next year, my class was moved down to that big room. But I was puzzled. This group of kids was different from last year's class. When these kids came into the classroom, they immediately began racing back and forth across the room. It was hard to settle them down.

Then I began to look at the environment, and I realized what had happened. The kids weren't any different than last year's. What *was* different was the room. I began to look at it from a child's perspective. It was like a gymnasium to them, and it invited running. The solution to my problem was easy. I blocked the "raceway." I moved a table and chairs into the open space. I rearranged the bookshelf, easels, sand table, and other furniture so the temptation to run was no longer a factor. My class was much more controlled.

Is your room too crowded? If a child has to walk through the book corner to get to the blocks, the children who are peacefully looking at books will be disturbed. They'll get frustrated. Then they'll be tempted to trip or hit the children walking through. Some children who are crowded do what their instincts tell them to do: They push. It's their way of communicating. They are saying, "Give me more space. You're crowding me."

Is your room age-appropriate? Are the tables and chairs the right size? Are there colorful pictures on the walls? Is the setting informal, so that it welcomes all kinds of learners?

Is your room neat but not sterile? A messy room will tell the children that the teacher doesn't care, so they won't care if they mess it up even more. But a room that's too neat is not inviting or comfortable. It makes kids feel like they can't do anything for fear of messing something up.

Program

Does your schedule fit the needs of the children? Are they getting restless just when you've tried to settle them down for group time? Maybe you should change the time for your large group activity. Could they be hungry? Do you need to schedule a snack at this time? Is it time for something active? Is it time for a rest?

When do problems occur? Do they happen when you are changing from one activity to another? If so, you may need to think of ways to make the transition smoother. Could you make a "path" of masking tape the children follow from one center to another?

Do you have a plan for getting everyone's attention? Equip your classroom with some type of signal to use when you want to get everyone's attention. I use a bell. When I ring the bell, everyone is supposed to sit down where they are, "freeze," look at me, and listen. We even play this as a game, practicing it as a fun way to get everyone's attention. Other teachers use the lights, turning them off when everyone is to get quiet. Some teachers sing a simple song, and the children can join in.

Do you have enough activities? Do you have things planned for those kids who finish an activity quickly? Do you have enough variety in the activities you've chosen? Change the games, puzzles, and toys in the room from time to time to keep it interesting. Is class time fun? Are the activities enjoyable? Do you make choices available? Are you excited yourself? If you're not excited to come to class, the children will not be excited either.

Do you give the children tasks that they can achieve? Do they feel successful in class?

Are you consistent? If co-teachers and aides have different expectations, there will be problems. Changing your rules or your enforcement of the rules from week to week will cause problems too.

After the children know what is expected of them, they will often test you to see if the boundaries are going to hold. Don and Jeanne Elium, authors of *Raising a Son,* write that children want to know "Who's the boss . . . what are the rules. . . and are you going to enforce them?"[5] Consistent enforcement of the boundaries makes children feel secure. The teacher can be counted on to keep the classroom a safe and welcoming place.

It's a good idea to ask the children to help make the rules. Then they feel like this is indeed *their* classroom. They see themselves as valued decision makers. If the children make the rules, they are quicker to abide by them and to see that others in class do too. They may be more strict in making their rules than you would be, and you might want to soften their intensity.

Try to have only a few rules, and state them positively. For older children, write the rules on a chart and post it in your classroom. For younger children, you might use pictures as symbols to represent each rule. In my four-year-old class, we had four rules written on a poster in rebus form:

We are happy (designated with a smiley face) to help (shown by a hand print).

We are happy (smiley face) to share (a hand holding out an apple).

We are happy (smiley face) to love (shown by a heart).

We are happy (smiley face) to obey (shown by a big letter O).

We "read" these sentences at the beginning of each group time for several weeks.

Discipline in the Sunday School

In seminars around the country and the world, teachers tell me about undisciplined children who come to their classrooms. Some of these children have received very little discipline at home. Their needs are not being met, and that puts a strain on the Sunday school teachers.

Part of the problem is our society. As "child-rights" conscious as we seem to be, we are often blind to our lack of respect for the individual child. Adults can be very self-centered, with short-term goals of comfort, pleasure, and ease. Even Christians can get so focused on getting ourselves spiritually fed and healing our pains that we overlook the needs of our children.

Some people see children as "in the way." We put them into day care and preschool earlier and earlier. We think day care and preschool provide good "socialization" for our children. But the foundation is often missing: the security and trust, strength, and comfort that can come only from a close relationship with Mom and Dad.

So these emotionally hungry children come to our classes. What do they find? Many times they find a lack of love and care on the teacher's part. Misbehaving children are the hardest to love. Their behavior drives away the very thing they are trying to ask for.

Why are we Sunday school teachers inattentive? It's partly due to the limited time we have with the children. Many times we don't know them very well. How can we get to know them well in forty-five minutes once a week? Our inattention is partly due to the shortage of workers whose hearts are dedicated to children. Many teachers just try to "get through" the hour and "cover the material." Teaching is many times turned over to people who aren't trained. They enter the classroom with a survival mentality.

The Remedy

What can we do? The most important thing to do is pray. Pray that people's hearts will turn to children and that we will have loving and willing people to work with kids. Pray that the hearts of church leaders will turn to children. I've seen again and again that if there is an encouraging emphasis on children from the pulpit, the children's program grows and thrives. If children are not supported from the pulpit, the children's program will limp along and suffocate.

Teacher training can help. When we do get those wonderful volunteers, they need to be equipped to go to work in the classroom. They need to know what to expect and how to touch the lives of children. Untrained teachers usually burn out quickly. They have unsuccessful experiences in class, and many of them don't volunteer again.

One remedy might be to have your teachers "graduate" with the children. The teacher gets to know those particular kids: what motivates them, what they dislike, how they relate to each other, ways to keep misbehavior to a minimum with these kids. The teacher is dedicated to a relationship with those children and moves up with them as they grow. His influence with those children will reach much farther than it would if he only worked with them for a few months.

It might help to divide your church into small groups or family groups and include the children. Then they develop relationships with other adults. Parents can get help with parenting skills from older adults in their group.

Provide parenting classes. Most parents are interested in getting help in parenting. If you suspect that the children in your Sunday school program are not being trained at home, then offer parents a way to grow in their training skills. You will not only have helped your classes, you will have helped parent-child relationships. That will be far more influential on the child than your class will.

Three blind men were walking excitedly down a road, traveling to a world famous bazaar. There they would smell the wonderful spices and feel the rolls of silks. They would hear the music of the pipers and buy sweet, cool fruit juices.

The blind men had not gone far when they came to an elephant standing in the middle of the road. The first blind man bumped into the elephant's trunk. When he felt it, he declared that they had stumbled across a snake. He concluded that they must have come upon a snakes' den. They would have to circle around until they were sure they had avoided the snakes. Then they could go on their way.

But the second blind man was feeling the elephant's tall, wide side. He insisted that they had bumped into a wall. They would definitely have to climb over it.

The third blind man had his arms around one of the elephant's legs. He announced that he had run into a tree. He decided that they must be entering a dense jungle. They would have to make their way slowly and carefully through the trees.

The blind men began to argue. None of them could agree on what they had bumped into or how they should proceed. Finally, because they could not agree, they just turned around and went back home.

That's sometimes the way it is with the question of discipline. We are going along our merry way when we bump into a child who misbehaves. We are unsure of why he is misbehaving and we are unsure of what to do about it. Different experts have different opinions. What do we do? Sometimes we just turn around and don't deal with it at all.

There are actually many things you can do. The next chapter will give some specific suggestions for dealing with discipline problems.

On the Other Side of the Coin

Correcting Misbehavior

Four year old: Daniel's grandmother died.
Mom: How sad! Did you tell him you're sorry?
Four year old: I didn't do it!

Psychiatrist Alfred Adler studied behavior and misbehavior in children. He said that a misbehaving child is a discouraged child.[1] Remember the discussion of children's needs in chapter 2? **S**ecurity, **O**ptimism, **S**ignificance, **B**elonging, **E**xploration, **A**ppreciation of childhood, **R**elationship. The S.O.S. Bear was a reminder of what happens when children's needs are not met. They send us an S.O.S. signal by their behavior.

Dr. Rudolf Dreikurs also devoted much of his time to studying behavior in children. He identified four goals of misbehavior.[2] L. Tobin, in his book *What Do You Do With a Child Like This?*, shares with us how to identify the goal by looking at our reaction.[3]

Does the behavior	The child's goal is
annoy you?	attention.
anger you?	power.
hurt you?	revenge.
make you despair?	showing his inadequacy.

In the classroom, it may not be you the child is annoying. He may be annoying another child. He wants that child's attention. Perhaps he wants to play with that child and he doesn't know how. Or maybe he's making another child angry. He wants to be in control of the situation. Maybe he's hurt another child, getting back at that child for something the child did to him. Or maybe he's not even trying, saying, "I can't," or shying away from the activities. He's showing his feeling of inadequacy.

We have a choice. We can deal with the behavior, or we can deal with the need that prompted that behavior. Dealing with the behavior is the short-term solution. It will work momentarily, but if the need has not been met, the behavior will resurface. Dealing with the need means that when the need has been met, the goal is no longer there and the behavior will no longer be necessary.

Looking at the Big Picture

If the child's goal is attention, it is the need for relationship that fuels that goal. What can we do to help meet that need? Give the child attention. But we have to do it when he is not exhibiting the misbehavior. We make sure we give him positive attention at other times.

If the child's goal is power, it is the need for belonging that fuels that goal. Part of belonging is having responsibilities, being in charge of something that contributes to the welfare of the group. What can we do to help meet the need for belonging? Give the child a job to do in the classroom that will allow him to lead in a constructive way. But he must also know that as a member of the group, he has to go by the rules of the group.

Another possible need that could fuel the goal of power is the need for security. The child wants to feel safe. That means being in control so he can protect himself. Or he pushes the boundaries to see who is in control. He will feel better helping set the rules for the group. In any case, knowing that there are rules that will be consistently enforced helps him feel secure.

If the child's goal is revenge, it is the need for significance that fuels that goal. He needs to feel respected, because people who respect him and think he's important will not hurt him. He is trying to communicate to others how it feels to be hurt. What can we do to help meet the need for significance? We can respect the child and make sure he knows he's significant to us. Then we can make sure we take time to discuss, with the child and the class, ways to show we care about others. Talk about how to treat each other with respect, including the Golden Rule, "Do to others as you would have them do to you" (Luke 6:31).

If the child's goal is to show inadequacy, it is the need for optimism, exploration and appreciation of childhood that fuels that goal. Somewhere the child has become convinced that he can't achieve. Look back at the negative sides of Erikson's tasks at each age level. This child feels shame or guilt or inferiority. He feels incompetent. How can we help the child meet his need for optimism, exploration, and appreciation for his childhood? We can encourage him. When he begins to step out tentatively and explore his abilities, we can be encouraging and nonjudgmental. We can be content to let the child be who he is at his age and not expect him to act or achieve on levels that would be expected of an older child.

Correction

Even though we may be meeting the child's needs, that does not mean the behavior will immediately stop. This is a process. We may have to work on both the short-term and long-term problems at the same time. That is, we may need to work on ministering to the child's need, while also working on the behavior. The child may feel good about the way his needs are starting to be met, but he may feel unhappy about having to control himself in the area of his behavior.

One of the problems that adults have is that we have been intimidated by the behaviors of children. If we are intimidated, we can be manipulated. Fred Gosman, in his book *Spoiled Rotten: Today's Children and How to Change Them,* says, "We're paralyzed at the thought of a child being unhappy."[4] Sometimes we will have to correct children and allow them to be unhappy for awhile.

It's in the area of correction that we are often baffled. What specifically do I do to deal with this problem? What are my options?

Think

Let's say you have a behavior problem in your classroom. What do you do now? Dr. Stanley Turecki, author of *The Difficult Child,* says that the first thing to do is detach yourself. Don't become emotionally involved, but be neutral.[5] Grace Mitchell says to hesitate.[6] This gives you time to weigh what's happening. (You would not hesitate if the safety of children is involved, as in the case of biting, hitting, or throwing. Then you immediately give attention to a hurt child and move the misbehaving child away from the situation.)

Now think. What did the child intend to do? Is this really misbehavior, or does this behavior bother me because the child's learning style is different than mine? Is it unusual for the child to act this way? Could he be getting sick? Could he be having problems at school or at home?

If you or the child are angry, you need this "think time" so you can both cool off. You might want to send the child to a time-out, cooling-off place, saying, "We'll discuss this after we have had time to calm down."

If you need the child to tell you about the situation, say, "Tell me what happened." If you ask, "Why did you do that?" you probably won't get the information you need. Children don't usually know why they did it. It also makes it easy for them to blame someone else.

Discuss the child's behavior with him in private if possible. Tell him why the behavior is unacceptable, or ask him to tell you. Encourage him, "You can do better than this. I know you will do better next time." Tell him what the consequences will be for that behavior. Sometimes you can ask the child what options he might suggest for consequences.

Hemfelt and Warren write, "Actions invite consequences. By giving a child a choice of actions, each with its attendant consequences, we can reinforce the cardinal rule: What happens to you is up to you."[7]

Next, choose your course of action and follow through.

Act

Nothing will ruin your discipline plan quicker than failing to impose the consequences. Not following through is an open invitation to misbehavior.

There is one exception to this that you might want to try occasionally. An excellent teacher introduced this concept to me. It's the idea of mercy. First, the children have to know you are consistent about enforcing the rules of your classroom. Then, if a child misbehaves and knows what he deserves, sometimes you can say, "You know what should happen now. But I'm going to give you mercy. I'm going to give you something you don't deserve, because God gave all of us mercy when Jesus died for our sins."

You have several options to choose from when you want to help change a child's behavior. Of course, you don't want to be going down the list and trying to decide what to do when you're already in the heat of battle. Choose a few of these ahead of time. Some of these are methods that you can implement as motivators for good behavior before misbehavior occurs.

- **Praise.** Watch for good behavior and reinforce it with positive comments and specific praise. "You knew just how to do that!" "Great job on your project!" "You put the trash in the trash can! What would we do without you?" "You were very persistent!" "I'm so glad you are part of our class!"

- **Redirect the child.** This works especially well with younger children and is used almost exclusively for children younger than eighteen months old. Distract their attention to something else. Show them what else they might do. Physically move them if you need to.
- **Time-out.** This is perhaps one of the most commonly used consequences. It is a time to cool off. It was originally called "time out from positive reinforcement." That means that the child gets no attention during time out. If he gets up, physically take him back to the chair. Start timing all over again. If he is loud, he has to sit until he is quiet, then the timing starts again.

If you choose time-out, have a timer in your room for this purpose. A good way to decide how long to leave a child in time-out is to think of his age. Usually a child can handle as many minutes as his age in years. A five year old can handle five minutes. A four year old can take four minutes, and so on. Time-out can be started at about eighteen months. At that age, an assistant in class may have to hold the child gently but firmly without talking.

- **Child's choice time-out.** If you are working with a child who gets "revved up" and if you are able to communicate with him about the feelings he has when he starts to get out of control, you can make a quiet, alone space available to him. This would be a place where he can go to be by himself to calm down. He can learn to choose this time-out himself when he feels like he's starting to lose control.
- **Removal from the group.** This is similar to time-out. The child is sent to a specific place and is told specifically what he may do. His task could be reading a book, or it could be the behavior he is doing to disturb or annoy the group, depending on what that misbehavior is. He is told that when he is ready to behave (state the specific behavior), he may return to the group and join the activity.
- **Removal of material or privileges.** If a child can't use the glitter without tossing it in the air, then the glitter will be taken away, and he loses the right to work with glitter. If a

child throws the blocks, then he loses the right to play in the block center. The key to remember is to make sure the privilege taken away connects in a natural way to the behavior.

• **Natural consequences.** These are consequences that happen without your interference. For example, if he keeps leaning his chair backward and he falls, he has experienced the natural consequence. You will not need to point it out or say anything about it. (In this case, I would consider whether this child's learning style is informal, and I would think about replacing the chairs with beanbags.) Of course, you don't want to rely on natural consequences if the consequence would seriously hurt children.

• **Logical consequences.** These are consequences chosen and put into effect by the teacher. Let's say, for example, that you have a child who always squirts out puddles of glue whenever you have a project. You show him the way to use the glue, but he doesn't change his behavior. After watching and thinking, you decide that this is not accidental. So the next time you have a project, everyone except that child is given glue. He is given tape instead.

• **Incentives.** These are tangible ways to motivate the child to choose acceptable behavior.

Reward charts. Make these simple. Make them fun. Change them often to keep interest. You can place stickers on a chart for good behavior. Or draw smiley faces next to the children's names on a chart. In one of my large classes, I had a successful "mouse chart." Each child had a felt mouse on a large felt board. If a child misbehaved, I took down his mouse. At the end of each class time, I placed a yellow piece of felt (the cheese) next to each mouse that was still on the board. When a child collected four pieces of cheese by his mouse, he got a prize.

This brings us to the subject of rewards for good behavior. Some people refuse to give rewards because they feel that they are bribes. But a bribe is payment that someone receives in return for going against his conscience. Rewards are not bribes.

Rewards can be stickers, hand stamps, coupons, pizza points, ice cream points, pennies collected in a jar, or miscellaneous prizes. One thing to remember is that the younger the child, the shorter time there should be between the proper behavior and the reward, or between the misbehavior and the consequence. If a two year old has to wait to collect four pieces of cheese for his mouse, he will soon give up.

Connect the dots chart. Decide what the reward will be: ice cream coupon, fast food coupon, a pair of sunglasses. Draw that item in dot-to-dot form. Make one copy of it for each child. They can connect the dots, moving ahead one dot for each good behavior or for each class time that has been completed with acceptable behavior. As soon as each child completes his dot-to-dot, he gets his prize.

"Let your light shine." Bring a small lamp to class. Turn it on at the beginning of class time. If it stays on for the whole class time, everyone gets a prize. But if a child misbehaves, he turns the light off. It doesn't get turned back on until the beginning of the next class time. This incentive can be connected to the concept of "Let your light shine" (Matthew 5:16).

Earning tickets. Get a roll of tickets or make them by cutting colored paper. Keep them close to you and give children tickets for displaying good behavior. They can lose tickets for bad behavior. They can earn treats by collecting a certain number of tickets.[8]

Penny cups. For each child, set out a cup with five pennies in it (or some other token or prize). Agree with the children that they can take home the contents of the cup when class is over. For misbehavior, a penny (or prize) comes out. For another misbehavior, another one comes out. Whatever the child has left in his cup, he takes home.

Pocket cards. This is used for older children. Get one small envelope for each child. Cut the flaps off the envelopes and glue the fronts of the envelopes to a piece of poster board. Write one child's name on each envelope. Place five colored index cards in each envelope: one each of white, blue, yellow, orange, and red. Place them in that color order with the white at the front.

If the child misbehaves, he must pull out the card in front and place it at the back of the other cards. When the blue card is showing at the front, this is a warning. When the yellow card shows, he sits out for one activity. The orange card in front means he sits out and writes a letter to his parents telling them what he has done. You take the letter when he's finished and mail it during the week. The red card means he is taken out of class to his parents. Start the cards over with the white in front at the beginning of each class.

Teachers who have used this system say it works well. Rarely do their students get past the warning stage.

- **Counting down.** For younger children, counting "1, 2, 3," after telling them what to do gives them time to choose to comply. Pause a second or two after each number. If you are working with a child on a particular behavior, you might even be able to start counting without saying anything else. "John, 1, 2, 3." He will know that you've seen what he's doing and that he'd better stop.
- **A sense of humor.** Sometimes responding humorously will defuse the situation and get the desired behavior. Sometimes young children say "No" just to make the statement that they are becoming independent. Sometimes I just smile, reach down and tickle them, and say in a playful tone, "No? What do you mean, no?" Then I repeat the instructions, and often the child complies.

Or you can tell a child, "Throw your grumpies (or loud voice or wigglies or grabbies or wrestles) outside. They'll wait for you there and you can get them again when you go back out the door." Then you can pretend to throw them out. If the child is young, you can even walk with him to the door, pretend to put the grumpies by the door and say, "Stay there!" and come back in without them.

- **Class meetings.** Having "meetings" for a few minutes during class once a month will help to keep everyone aware of the rules. Let the kids tell you if they are having any

Pocket Cards

problems. Let them help you decide if rules need to be changed. If there are behavior problems, the children themselves can suggest solutions.

You should feel free to discuss behavior problems with the child's parents. Parents are usually glad to be consulted. It all depends on how you approach it. Don't tell them what a bad child they have. Instead, tell them you're learning how to work with their child, and ask if they have found a method that is effective at home that you might use in the classroom. If this is a child with hyperactivity, a learning disability, or another physical reason for behaving the way he does, the parent is probably your best source for information about how to work with him.

As God Does

Several years ago, a new little boy came to my four-year-old class. As we gathered for the last group time of the evening, I noticed that he held one hand tightly closed and had a very guilty look on his face.

"Ted," I said, "you need to show me what's in your hand."

Ted did nothing. I led the children in another song.

"Ted," I said, "I need to see what's in your hand."

Ted did nothing. Periodically during the closing group time, I asked to see what he held. He didn't budge. I thought, *He's new. He's not ever going to want to come back to class. He'll hate me for this.* But I couldn't let him get away with taking something he knew he shouldn't have.

When Ted's mother came, I told her I needed to see what he held. She talked to him, and finally he opened his hand. He had been holding the cap to a cheap ball point pen. "Thank you for showing me," I said. "You may keep it."

I felt bad about it, but I knew that if I had let him go, he would have felt like he'd gotten away with something. I could tell that he already felt guilty.

But Ted came back again and again. And he didn't hate

me. He would hug me whenever he saw me in the halls at church, even after he was too old to come to my class.

What does God say about misbehaving? "When people sin, you should forgive and comfort them, so they won't give up in despair. You should make them sure of your love for them" (2 Corinthians 2:7, 8, CEV). "Do as God does. . . . Let love be your guide" (Ephesians 5:1).

Reasonable, responsible, consistent, encouraging, and loving. That's our goal in discipline.

The Growing TEACHER

What About Me?

The Spiritual Needs of the Teacher

"Never give up.
Keep on trying until you get it right."
—Five year old

The little black box is opened. The button is pushed. The tape begins to play. "Your mission, should you decide to accept it. . . ." The impossibly difficult mission is described. Then the tape self-destructs. After all the information is given, the important question remains, "Should you decide to accept it?"

It was pointed out earlier that going into the classroom to teach children is a bit like going into a mission field. It's like going into a different culture. If you're going, you should go prepared. You'll have ups and downs, but the ultimate rewards for your dedication will be far beyond what you could imagine.

So grab your imaginary backpack, and let's fill it with what you will need to keep yourself nourished on this mission: **Committed Love**.

C Come to the Feast

"The kingdom of heaven is like a king who prepared a wedding banquet for his son. He sent his servants to those who had been invited to the banquet to tell them to come, but they refused to come" (Matthew 22:2, 3).

You cannot lead a child to somewhere you've never been. God has prepared a spiritual feast for you that starts long before you get to Heaven. He wants Jesus to be the bread of *your* life. He wants to be *your* living water. He wants to be *your* way, *your* truth, *your* life.

Don't be content just to know *about* him. Seek *him*. Pursue *him*. Mary did. Martha was busy, but Mary did not leave Jesus. "Come near to God and he will come near to you" (James 4:8).

0 One-on-One Time With God

If coming to the feast is your goal, one-on-one time with God is the way to get there. One-on-one time includes your private Bible reading, meditation, and prayer. It is not done in preparation for a class. It's a special time to be with your Father. It's a time to talk with him and a time to let him teach you. "Your word is a lamp to my feet and a light for my path" (Psalm 119:105). Can you imagine turning on the lights in your house only one night a week? You'd end up with bruises and sprains from bumping into tables and tripping over chairs. Some of life's bumps and bruises come because we ignore the "lamp" of God's Word. God told his people, "Take to heart all the words I have solemnly declared to you this day. . . . They are not just idle words for you—they are your life" (Deuteronomy 32:46, 47).

If you need help learning how to pray, start with the psalms. Pray them yourself, making them apply to you. "Father, I want to be blessed, so I try not to walk in the counsel of the wicked. Make me wise, so I can tell good counsel from bad. Don't let me stand in the way of sinners. Forgive me for times I've sat in the seat of mockers" (prayed from Psalm 1:1). If you pray one psalm a day, it will take you 150 days. Many psalms will last you for more than one day. So go into training.

Something else to help your prayer life is to go through your Bible, highlighting the places where someone talks to God. See how people talked to him. They can be examples for you.

One thing that helped me was to write down categories of things I wanted to pray about. Then I assigned each category to a day. Every prayer included a time of thanksgiving, praise, and prayer for my immediate family. In addition to that, I spent time in prayer for the category that day. For example, I prayed for my extended family on Monday. On Tuesday I prayed for the sick. On Wednesday I prayed for salvation for people I knew who hadn't committed their lives to Jesus yet. On Thursday I prayed for our country. On Friday I prayed for missionaries and foreign countries.

These suggestions are just springboards to get you talking in meaningful ways to your Father. You will soon be talking to him spontaneously just as you'd talk to any friend who was standing nearby. Then you'll leave the springboards behind and dive in!

M Maturity Is Your Goal

"I press on to take hold of that for which Christ Jesus took hold of me" (Philippians 3:12).

Earlier we took a brief look at Erikson's stages of development in adults.[1] Let's take a closer look now. Erikson says that after the stage of developing our identity, we go through a period of *transition*. This generally occurs in our twenties. We develop either *intimacy* or *isolation*. Intimacy develops from having a friend whose friendship never wavers, even when that friend knows everything about us, including our deepest secrets. This intimacy results in the strength of *love*. At this time, our faith grows in cycles of reflecting and recommitting.[2] We evaluate our faith and then recommit to a stronger walk with the Lord. If intimacy does not develop, then we live in *isolation*.

From our thirties through our sixties, we are in a stage of *generativity* or *stagnation*. This can be a period of high productivity, or not. Generativity also has to do with generations because part of the reason we produce has to do with providing for the next generation. The strength that grows out of this time is *care*. At this stage, faith includes accepting hardships as part of life. And our relationship with God should be growing deeper.

The next stage is older adulthood. According to Erikson, during this stage we develop either a sense of *integrity* or a sense of *despair*. Integrity comes with satisfaction in the fullness of life. Despair comes with regrets and loss of hope. Faith now includes understandings that come from our own experiences as we have walked with God. The strength that comes from these years is the strength of *wisdom*.

All through these years, we should be continuing our growth into maturity.

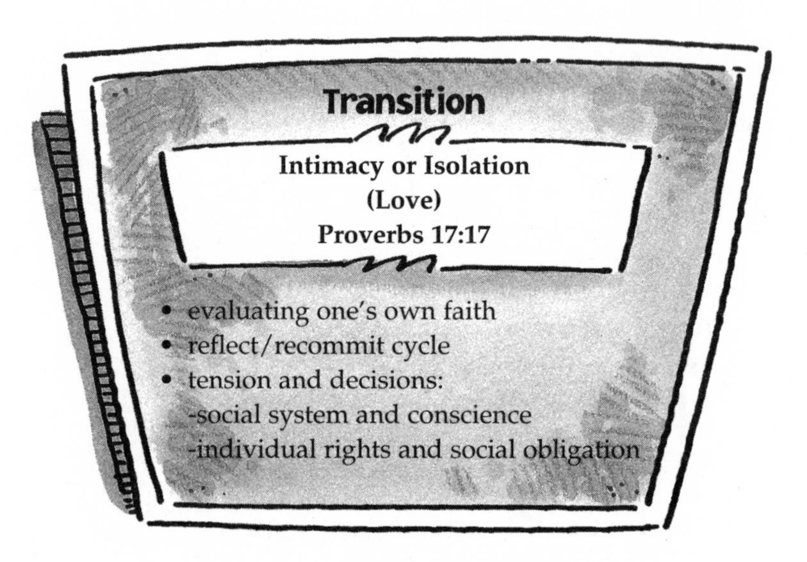

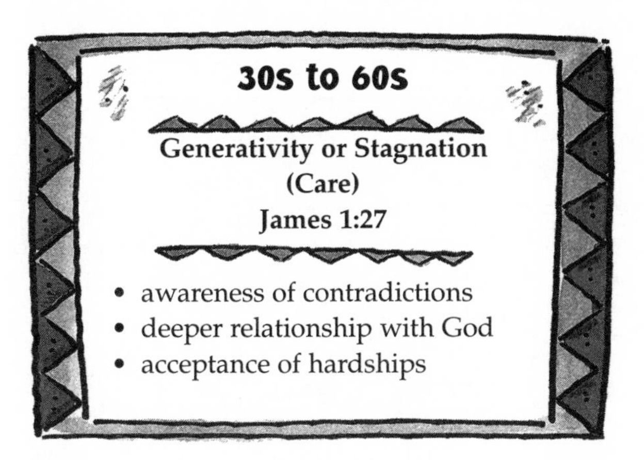
30s to 60s
Generativity or Stagnation
(Care)
James 1:27
• awareness of contradictions
• deeper relationship with God
• acceptance of hardships

Older Adulthood
Integrity or Despair
(Wisdom)
Proverbs 8:11
• encompassing life's experiences
• selfless passion
• "They will still bear fruit" (Psalm 92).
• "Even to your old age . . . I will sustain you" (Isaiah 46:4).

There is no retirement from being in the Lord's kingdom. "The righteous will flourish like a palm tree, they will grow like a cedar of Lebanon. . . . They will still bear fruit in old age, they will stay fresh and green, proclaiming, 'The Lord is upright; he is my Rock, and there is no wickedness in him'" (Psalm 92:12-15).

Are you discontent with where you are spiritually? Good. Be discontent. Use that discontentment to motivate you to press on. We will still be "pressing on toward the goal" as long as we have life on this earth.

M Mind That's Transformed

"Do not conform any longer to the pattern of this world, but be transformed by the renewing of your mind. Then you will be able to test and approve what God's will is—his good, pleasing and perfect will" (Romans 12:2). We must learn to see things from God's perspective, not from the world's perspective.

The first and greatest commandment, Jesus said, is "Love the Lord your God with all your heart and with all your soul and with all your *mind*" (Matthew 22:37, italics added). There's no halfhearted love here. This is an "undivided heart" (Psalm 86:11). It's an undivided mind. When you're in love with God, everything else falls into place. "The mind controlled by the Spirit is life and peace" (Romans 8:6).

I Include Pain and Problems

The very fact of putting a sentence about having pain and problems right after a sentence about life and peace shows the transformed perspective of the mind controlled by the Spirit. To the world's way of thinking, pain and problems bring the opposite of peace. But God gives us life and peace *during* the pain and problems. In fact, God works in our pain and problems and makes everything work out for good. Jesus said, "I have told you these things, so that in me you may have peace. In this world you will have trouble. But take heart! I have overcome the world!" (John 16:33).

T Teachable Spirit

Benjamin Franklin once said, "He who cannot obey, cannot command." In the same way, someone who can't be taught, can't teach. It's not unusual for the teacher to learn more than those he teaches. Be open to learning from your teaching experience. God has rich blessings in store for you. Jesus said, "Take my yoke upon you and learn from me" (Matthew 11:29). What will happen when we learn from Jesus? "You will find rest for your souls" (Matthew 11:29). There's that peace again.

T Trust

"Trust in the Lord with all your heart and lean not on your own understanding; in all your ways acknowledge him, and he will make your paths straight" (Proverbs 3:5, 6). As we said in chapter 3, God didn't ask us to understand. He asked us to trust.

When the Israelites faced the Red Sea with the enemy army hot on their trail, they began to cry out. "It would have been better to stay in Egypt," they said. But Moses told them, "Do not be afraid. Stand firm and you will see the deliverance the Lord will bring you today. . . . The Lord will fight for you; you need only to be still" (Exodus 14:13, 14). They did not understand, but Moses was asking them to trust.

"I am the Lord, your God, who takes hold of your right hand and says to you, 'Do not fear; I will help you'" (Isaiah 41:13).

E Energy That God Provides

Teaching is time consuming and energy consuming. Paul says he worked "struggling with all [God's] energy, which so powerfully works in me" (Colossians 1:29).

It's been said that God doesn't call the equipped, he equips the called. God doesn't give us a task to do and then not give us all we need to accomplish that task. Hebrews 11 tells about people like Gideon, Samson, Samuel, and David "whose weakness was turned to strength" (Hebrews 11:32-34). We think of these people as strong, but they were just as weak as we are. When they let God use them for his purposes, they became strong.

D Don't Be a One-Man Show

Have you ever watched geese fly? Each goose makes an "uplift" of air when it flaps its wings. This uplift helps the geese that are following it. So when the whole flock flies in "V" formation, it has a much greater flying range than if each goose flew by itself. If a goose falls out of formation, it will feel the drag of the resistant air and will soon join the flock again. When the lead goose gets tired, it leaves the front and moves back in the group. Another goose takes its place. From watching geese, we can learn some good lessons about working as a team.

In his letter to the Ephesians, Paul shows how the church is a body. All the parts work together. "From him the whole body, joined and held together by every supporting ligament, grows and builds itself up in love, as each part does its work" (Ephesians 4:16). There's an old saying, "Many hands make light work." The load is lighter if there's someone to help you carry it.

There's something else that's interesting about geese. The geese that are farther back in the formation honk to encourage the geese in the lead to keep moving. And if a goose gets sick or wounded, two other geese leave the flock to follow it down. They try to help and protect the hurting goose. They'll stay with the hurt goose until it dies or can fly again. Then they'll fly out with another flock of geese, or they'll catch up with their own flock.

Paul wrote, "Encourage one another and build each other up. . . . Encourage the timid, help the weak, be patient with everyone" (1 Thessalonians 5:11, 14).

L Look at Jesus

What makes us get discouraged? One reason is focusing on ourselves and the world around us instead of on Jesus. Peter got to do something no one else had ever done. He got to walk on water. As long as he was looking at Jesus, he was fine. It was when he stopped looking at Jesus that he began to sink. "Let us fix our eyes on Jesus, the author and perfecter of our faith. . . . Consider him . . . so that you will not grow weary and lose heart" (Hebrews 12:2, 3).

Second Corinthians 3:17–4:2 shows us three other things that keep us from "losing heart." "Now the Lord is the Spirit, and where the Spirit of the Lord is, there is freedom. And we, who with unveiled faces all reflect the Lord's glory, are being transformed into his likeness with ever-increasing glory, which comes from the Lord, who is the Spirit. Therefore, since through God's mercy we have this ministry, we do not lose heart. Rather, we have renounced secret and shameful ways; we do not use deception, nor do we distort the word of God."

These verses show that one way to keep from losing heart is realizing that our ministry is to reflect the Lord's glory. We can only do this by looking his direction.

Another thing these verses teach that will keep us from getting discouraged is realizing that it's through God's mercy that we have our ministry. God is not joining in with our work. Instead, we are joining in with his work. We're not in charge. God is.

One other thing will help us not to give up: renouncing hidden or unconfessed sin. Guilt can be a heavy burden. It can slow us down or make us give up completely. God doesn't intend for us to bear the burden of guilt. Jesus died to take our guilt away. He volunteered to be punished for all our sins. So when Jesus died, God erased our sins. And he continues to erase our sins. So confess them, renounce them, and press on.

O Optimism

We should read the eighth chapter of Romans at least once a month. We'd be reminded that we should have no reason to ever live without joy the rest of our lives. The chapter starts out saying, "Therefore, there is now no condemnation for those who are in Christ Jesus."

Here are some other highlights:

"For you did not receive a spirit that makes you a slave again to fear, but you received the Spirit of sonship. And by him we cry, 'Abba, Father'" (v. 15).

"I consider that our present sufferings are not worth comparing with the glory that will be revealed in us" (v. 18).

"The Spirit himself intercedes for us with groans that words cannot express" (v. 26).

"We know that in all things God works for the good of those who love him" (v. 28).

"If God is for us, who can be against us?" (v. 31).

"We are more than conquerors through him who loved us" (v. 37).

"For I am convinced that neither death nor life, neither angels nor demons, neither the present nor the future, nor any powers, neither height nor depth, nor anything else in all creation, will be able to separate us from the love of God that is in Christ Jesus our Lord" (v. 39).

Optimistic? Optimism should be an understatement! This good news should make us laugh, sing, praise, dance, and cry tears of joy!

V Vision

We need to be able to see things not as what they are, but as what they can become. That's seeing with God's vision.

Romans 4:17 says that God "calls things that are not as though they were." Abram was ninety-nine when God renamed him "Abraham" saying, "You will be the father of many nations" (Genesis 17:4). Abraham didn't have any children yet, but God saw what he would become.

Jesus looked at Simon and said, "You will be called Cephas (which, when translated, is Peter)" (John 1:42). Peter was an impulsive man, changing his mind in order to please (John 13:9) or to save his skin (John 18:25) or to avoid criticism (Galatians 2:12). But Jesus looked at what Peter would become: a rock.

Jesus turned water into wine. He turned a basket of loaves and fish into a feast for more than five thousand. Surely he is able to take the humble lives we offer him and turn them into far more than we ever dreamed. God "is able to do immeasurably more than all we ask or imagine, according to his power that is at work within us" (Ephesians 3:20).

E Enter as a Child

We began looking at Committed Love by hearing God say, "Come to the feast." But we must enter by becoming like a child. "I tell you the truth, unless you change and become like little children, you will never enter the kingdom of heaven" (Matthew 18:3).

What does it mean to become like a little child? A little child is willing to believe. A little child is humble and in awe of strength. To him, his daddy can do anything. We look at God through the eyes of the child. God is our daddy. God loves us very much. And he is strong enough to do anything. "Nothing is impossible with God" (Luke 1:37).

A little child knows he's weak. But God says, "My power is made perfect in weakness" (2 Corinthians 12:9). A little child is willing to take risks. He says, "I can do it." Paul said, "I can do everything through him who gives me strength" (Philippians 4:13).

Committed love. Your committed love for children

starts with his committed love for you. God offers you unchanging grace, unfailing love, and undeniable mercies. The only thing that can get in the way is an unyielding heart.

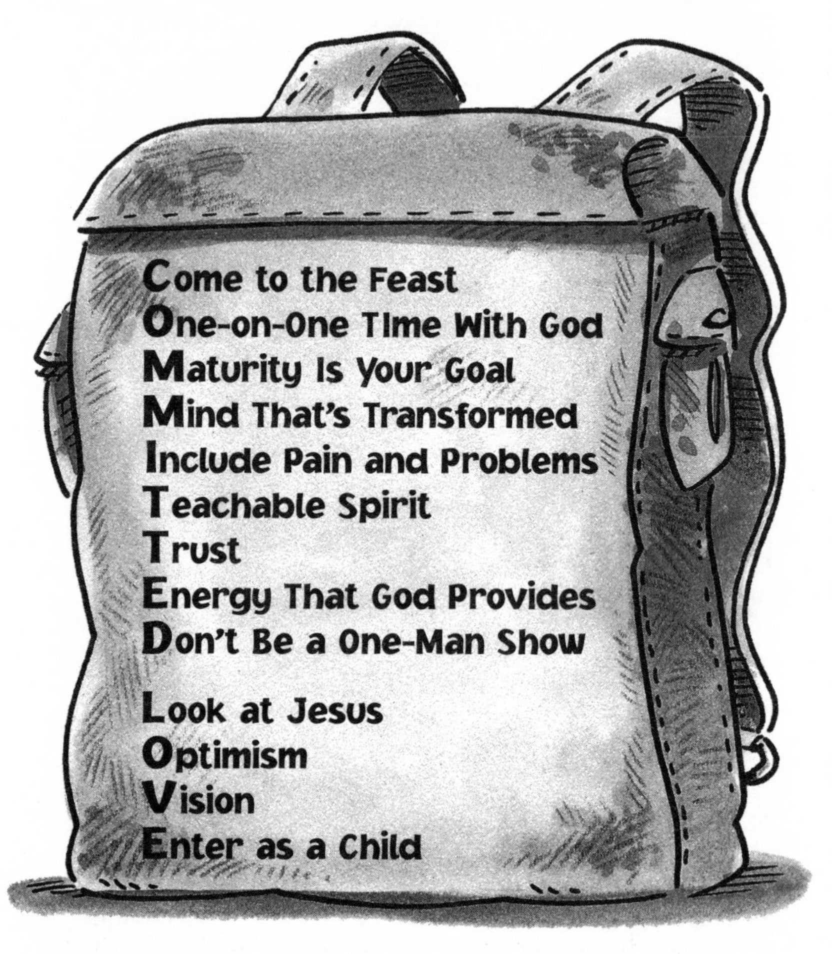

Your Turn

When my niece was a preschooler, she asked her daddy, "When you die, do you go into the Bible?" She knew the Bible told stories of God's people who had died. Maybe our stories went in there too.

Bible stories give us glimpses of a magnificent time line. From Adam to Noah to Abraham, Isaac, and Jacob. From Moses to David to Daniel. From Mary and Joseph to Peter, Paul, and the apostle John. And history rolls on. The time line that began with Adam and Eve runs through history, even to our time today. An ancient heritage and story continues to be woven. It is our privilege to be a part of this story too.

We stand on the time line in an age of precocious children, an age of change, an age of anxiety, an age of contrasts. Sometimes it's exciting. Sometimes it's discouraging. But Isaiah said, "He will be the sure foundation for your times" (Isaiah 33:6).

What a relief it is to know that throughout an age of change, God never changes. He is steadfast and faithful. James wrote that the Father "does not change like shifting shadows" (James 1:17). And the writer of Hebrews said, "Jesus Christ is the same yesterday and today and forever" (Hebrews 13:8).

Throughout an age of anxiety, our God gives us peace that surpasses understanding (Philippians 4:7).

In an age when children are pushed to grow up, our Lord told us to change and "become like little children" (Matthew 18:3).

In an age of conflict between light and dark, "The light shines in the darkness and the darkness has not overcome it" (John 1:5, RSV).

There is a place for each one of us on the time line. You are unique. God prepared a place for you on the time line, and he prepared you to fill that place. Your place is no less important than the place that Joseph was called to fill, or the place of David or Daniel or Ruth or Dorcas or Lydia. You are important.

There was once an old Hasidic Jewish leader named Zusia. He had many followers. One morning, when Zusia joined his followers, they saw that his eyes were red and swollen as if he'd been crying.

"Zusia," they said. "What is wrong?"

Zusia wailed. "I have learned what the angels will ask me one day."

His followers were amazed that any question put to their beloved leader could be so disturbing. "What will they ask you?" said his followers.

"I have learned," said Zusia, "that the angels will not ask me, 'Zusia, why have you not been a Moses, leading your people out of their Egypt?'"

Zusia's followers were still puzzled. "So what will the angels ask you?" they said.

"I have learned," said Zusia, "that the angels will not ask me, 'Zusia, why have you not been a Joshua, leading your people into their promised land?'"

Zusia's followers were even more curious. "So what will the angels ask you?" they said.

"I have learned," wailed Zusia, "that the angels will one day ask me, 'Zusia, why have you not been Zusia?'"

You have a place. You are significant. Listen to God's call. Commit yourself. Say, "Yes, Lord, whatever you want." And keep your eyes on him.

Like Peter, you've stepped out of the boat. Will you watch Jesus or the waves?

> May God "equip you with everything good for doing his will, and may he work in us what is pleasing to him, through Jesus Christ, to whom be glory for ever and ever. Amen."
>
> —Hebrews 13:21

Notes

Chapter 1

1. David Elkind, *The Hurried Child* (Reading, MA: Addison-Wesley, 1981).
2. C.D. Wright, "The Choice for Poetry," *The Writer*, May 1993.
3. *Zillions*, October/November 1993.
4. Robert Coles, "The Man Who Listens to Children," *Storytelling*, Fall 1992.

Chapter 2

1. Margit Feury, "Medical News," *Family Circle*, 16 July 1996.

Chapter 3

1. Robert Coles, *The Spiritual Life of Children* (Boston: Houghton Mifflin, 1990).
2. John W. Santrock, *Life-Span Development* (Dubuque, IA: Wm. C. Brown, 1989).
3. James W. Fowler, *Stages of Faith: The Psychology of Human Development and the Quest for Meaning* (San Francisco: Harper & Row, 1981).
4. Ibid.
5. William Sears, M.D., and Martha Sears, R.N., *The Discipline Book* (Boston: Little, Brown and Company, 1995).
6. Dorothy G. Singer and Tracey A. Revenson, *A Piaget Primer: How a Child Thinks* (New York: Penguin Books, 1978).
7. Howard Gardner, *The Unschooled Mind* (New York: HarperCollins, 1991).

Chapter 6

1. Raymond and Dorothy Moore, *Home Grown Kids* (Waco, TX: Word Books, 1981).
2. As quoted by Jim Trelease, *The Read-Aloud Handbook* (New York: Penguin Books, 1985).

Chapter 7

1. Stephen Jones, *Faith Shaping* (Valley Forge, PA: Judson Press, 1987).
2. Howard Gardner, *The Unschooled Mind* (New York: HarperCollins Publishers, 1991).

Chapter 8

1. Kevin Huggins, *Parenting Adolescents* (Colorado Springs, CO: Navpress, 1989).
2. Ibid.

Chapter 9

1. Bert Decker, *The Art of Communication* (Los Altos, CA: Crisp Publications, Inc., 1988). See also: B. Boylan, *What's Your Point?* (New York: Warner Books, 1988).
2. Robert Coles, "The Man Who Listens to Children," *Storytelling*, Fall 1992.
3. Dr. Robert Hemfelt and Dr. Paul Warren, *Kids Who Carry Our Pain* (Nashville, TN: Thomas Nelson, 1990).
4. Laura Ingalls Wilder, *On the Banks of Plum Creek* (New York: Harper & Row, 1937).
5. As quoted by Vernie Schorr, *Building Relations With Children* (International Center for Learning, 1978).

Chapter 10

1. Dr. Rita Dunn and Dr. Kenneth Dunn, *Teaching Elementary Students Through Their Individual Learning Styles* (Boston: Allyn and Bacon, 1992).
2. Marlene D. LeFever, *Learning Styles* (Colorado Springs, CO: David C. Cook, 1995).
3. Ibid.
4. Ibid.
5. Ibid.
6. Thomas Armstrong, *Seven Kinds of Smart* (New York: Penguin Books, 1993).
7. See also: Don Oldenburg, "A Hunger to Learn," *This World*, September 20, 1987.

Chapter 12

1. George Gerbner. Speech. 1990 National Congress on Storytelling.
2. Jim Trelease, *The Read-Aloud Handbook* (New York: Penguin Books, 1985).
3. Howard G. Hendricks, *The Seven Laws of the Teacher* (Atlanta: Walk Through the Bible Ministries, Inc., 1987).
4. Robert Coles, "The Man Who Listens to Children," *Storytelling*, Fall 1992.
5. Peninnah Schram, "Recalling Our Life Stories," *Yarnspinner*, February 1990.
6. Jack Maguire, *Creative Storytelling* (New York: McGraw-Hill, 1985).

Chapter 13

1. Mem Fox, *Wilfrid Gordon McDonald Partridge* (Brooklyn, NY: Kane/Miller Book Publishers, 1984).
2. Frank Smith, *Insult to Intelligence* (Portsmouth, NH: Heinemann, 1988).

Chapter 14

1. William Sears, M.D., and Martha Sears, R.N., *The Discipline Book* (Boston: Little, Brown and Company, 1995).
2. Grace Mitchell, *A Very Practical Guide to Discipline With Young Children* (Chelsea, MA: Telshare Publishing, 1982).
3. Bill Slonecker, M.D. Speech. 1993 Children's Pastors' Conference, Nashville, TN.
4. Grace Mitchell, *A Very Practical Guide to Discipline With Young Children* (Chelsea, MA: Telshare Publishing, 1982).
5. Don and Jeanne Elium, *Raising a Son: Parents and the Making of a Healthy Man* (Hillsboro, OR: Beyond Words Publishing, Inc., 1992).

Chapter 15

1. As quoted in: Rudolph Dreikurs, M.D., and Loren Grey, *The New Approach to Discipline* (New York: Penguin Books, 1968).
2. As quoted in: L. Tobin, *What Do You Do With a Child Like This?* (Duluth, MN: Whole Person Associates, 1991).
3. Ibid.
4. Fred Gosman, *Spoiled Rotten: Today's Children and How to Change Them* (New York: Villard, 1992).
5. Stanley Turecki, M.D., and Leslie Tonner, *The Difficult Child* (New York: Bantam Books, 1985).
6. Grace Mitchell, *A Very Practical Guide to Discipline With Young Children* (Chelsea, MA: Telshare Publishing, 1982).
7. Dr. Robert Hemfelt and Dr. Paul Warren, *Kids Who Carry Our Pain* (Nashville, TN: Thomas Nelson, 1990).
8. Some of these ideas are based on suggestions found in *The Discipline Book*. William Sears, M.D., and Martha Sears, R.N., *The Discipline Book* (Boston: Little, Brown and Company, 1995).

Chapter 16

1. John W. Santrock, *Life-Span Development* (Dubuque, Iowa: Wm. C. Brown, 1989).
2. James W. Fowler, *Stages of Faith: The Psychology of Human Development and the Quest for Meaning* (San Francisco: Harper & Row, 1981).